RUSH!

Beloved by millions, detested by thousands, here is an unbiased biography of a remarkable entertainer—the outrageous, outlandish, outspoken political pundit whose life is as controversial as his words.

RUSH!

The "most dangerous man in America," with a "talent on loan from God"

RUSH!

A mercilessly scathing verbal warrior on the airwaves, yet charming and shy in real life—a sensitive man who has cried in public . . . and whose favorite movie is "Love Story"

RUSH!

A former failed disc jockey from a tiny Midwestern town who has slept in the White House . . . and had a President carry his bags

RUSH!

RUSH!

MICHAEL ARKUSH

AVON BOOKS ◆ NEW YORK

RUSH! is an original publication of Avon Books. This work has never before appeared in book form.

AVON BOOKS
A division of
The Hearst Corporation
1350 Avenue of the Americas
New York, New York 10019

First Avon Books Printing: October 1993

AVON TRADEMARK REG. U.S. PAT. OFF. AND IN OTHER COUNTRIES, MARCA REGISTRADA, HECHO EN U.S.A.

Printed in the U.S.A.

RA 10 9 8 7 6 5 4 3 2 1

**With love to Pauletta,
whose beauty and strength are an inspiration
to everyone around her**

1

RUSH LIMBAUGH. THE NAME INSPIRES MILLIONS OF conservatives who see him as their intellectual Messiah, the only person courageous enough to speak the truth about a country losing its sanity.

Rush Limbaugh. The name irritates millions of liberals who see him as their nightmare of the 1990s, the horrifying example of what can happen in a free society when a man with a microphone seizes too much power.

Rush Limbaugh. Love him or loathe him, enshrine him or engage him, it's impossible to dismiss him. In five short years, since he arrived in New York during one of the city's most oppressive heat waves, he has become the hottest thing in radio. His show reaches eighteen million listeners on about 610 stations from coast to coast. The ratings for his half-hour television show surpass Arsenio and rival Leno.

So widespread is his popularity that dozens of restaurants across the country provide "Rush Rooms," in which patrons eat breakfast or lunch in respectful, almost God-fearing, silence to study their master's latest teachings from his throne on the EIB—Excellence in Broadcasting—Network in

Manhattan. He also has been a one-man industry, selling T-shirts, bumper stickers, mugs, and satin jackets as he took his conservative circus act from state to state, telling his followers the way things ought to be. His 1992 book, a regurgitation of his outspoken views, has remained a best-seller for months. A sequel is planned for a fall release. Many urge him to seek public office.

But who is Rush Limbaugh?

Is he an obese, forty-two-year-old failure as a disc jockey and husband out for revenge against the women who rejected him and the radio station managers who never let him be himself?

Is he a capitalist disguised as a moralist, interested primarily in the almighty buck and fortunate enough to have patented a product—old-fashioned conservatism with a hip, modern punchline—that can make him rich and famous?

Is he a deeply passionate right-wing thinker who sincerely wants to remake America into the land of his youth, before the liberals came to power and wrecked everything?

Or is he a disappointed son who has spent his life searching desperately for the approval of a demanding father whom he could never satisfy no matter what great things he accomplished?

Rush Limbaugh is a little bit of all those things, and more.

The "most dangerous man in America," as Rush Hudson Limbaugh III has been labeled, comes from one of the safest places on the planet. In the nation's heartland, sheltered from the urban unrest of the North and the polarizing prejudices of the South, he grew up in an environment and a time—the late 1950s and early 1960s—when every little boy could dream of becoming president or Mickey Mantle. His particular haven was a small Missouri town bordering the Mississippi River, about 100 miles south of St. Louis, called Cape Girardeau, or the "Cape" as its citizens prefer.

The Cape took almost a century to emerge from hibernation. The trouble was that until 1816, the only mode of transportation up the river was by keelboat, which kept most settlers away. Then, the steamboat made its historic debut, and within five years, several dozen were in operation on the Mississippi. Still, Cape Girardeau remained largely uncharted because it didn't benefit from the other momentous transportation innovation of the nineteenth century—the railroad.

Not until 1902 did the lines from St. Louis connect directly to the Cape. Within a decade, the town doubled in population to nearly ten thousand. With the railroad, which transported more freight than a steamboat, came businesses such as the Johnson Shoe Co. that, by 1910, employed as many as fourteen hundred people.

The town also went through a political metamorphosis, as well. Before the Civil War, Cape Girardeau belonged, in spirit, at least, to the South, and, yes, *the Democrats*. (Imagine, Rush Limbaugh could have become a Democrat!) There were approximately fifteen hundred slaves in the county, and the local newspaper, the *Western Eagle*, was run by a Confederate sympathizer, William

Dawson. Only the presence of a large contingent of German immigrants likely prevented the state from dropping out of the Union altogether.

The War, however, altered the town's destiny. When the Union troops arrived, they quickly built four forts and confiscated the newspaper. The Union printed its own propaganda sheet, cleverly maneuvering public opinion into its column, and Cape Girardeau would never be the same again. "That set the stage for the conservatism that continues through today," said Bob White, a history professor at Southeast Missouri State University, the Cape's hometown institution established in 1873 as the Normal School.

Another institution was beginning to carve out its own destiny at the same time. In neighboring Bollinger County, on a farm four miles south of Sedgewickville, the Limbaugh family made its home.

In 1891, the Limbaughs gave birth to a son, and called him Rush. Rush's father served on the board for the town's one-room elementary school. One day, because his father was sick—he later died of consumption at the age of forty-three—the board met at the farm. The meeting was held to resolve the difficulties the school's only teacher was having in trying to maintain discipline.

It had a lasting impression on the frightened boy. "I can remember it as well as if it happened yesterday," recalled Rush Limbaugh, Sr., in 1991, at the age of ninety-nine, in an interview with his hometown newspaper, the *Southeast Missourian*. "After a long period of discussion, my father said,

'If he [the teacher] can't keep order, he can't teach school.' I've remembered the word 'order' in that connection ever since."

There were many other lessons for the boy to learn outside the classroom. One day at school, word quickly spread that a fight would take place between two youngsters. "That day, at noon, a man came in from nowhere," Limbaugh remembered years later. "He got up after they had served dinner . . . and said, 'I came here today representing the law. I understood that there was going to be trouble here. I came to tell you there's not going to be any trouble here. Before anybody starts trouble in this crowd, he's got to go over me.' " The Limbaughs and The Law have been linked together ever since.

The family's long legacy of oratorical brilliance also originated with Grandpa Limbaugh. When he was only eleven, his sister, Lillie, who was a schoolteacher, brought him a volume of famous speeches to study. "I read it and began committing it to memory," he said. "I liked it. I liked to speak."

Through the decades, even into his late nineties, the old man could still give a damn good speech. Bill Stacy, who taught public speaking at Southeast Missouri State and later became the school's president, attended the swearing-in ceremony for Limbaugh's son, Stephen, when he became a federal district judge in the 1980s. (Stephen's son, Stephen Jr., incidentally, sits on the Missouri Supreme Court.)

"All the other justices came in with prepared remarks and read them very craftily," Stacy said.

"And then Rush Limbaugh [Sr.] stood up without a note and gave the most stirring oratory of the day."

After attending the Normal School and serving as an editor of the student newspaper, the *Capaha Arrow*, Limbaugh enrolled in law school at the University of Missouri. After only two years, he received his certificate in 1916, and started practicing law with the Cape Girardeau firm of Davis and Hardesty. "I agreed to pay them $50 for a chair and table in their office for that summer," he told the *Southeast Missourian*. "They gave me a number of accounts to collect for clients. Most of that summer was spent on making collections."

He had the option of going back to law school after that summer, but having to support a wife and baby, he remained in town and established his own practice. He didn't exactly conquer the Cape in that first year, earning less than $500. Unable to afford a car, he walked to work every day. In 1917, he started moonlighting as city attorney, prosecuting cases in municipal court on commission. "That was just a sideline for me," he said. "I was paid $3 for every conviction that I was able to secure." Defense attorneys joked that his true motivation for nailing convictions was to pick up the fee.

Limbaugh's stint as city attorney came to an end a year later when a commission form of government was instituted. But he couldn't stay out of city affairs forever. In 1924, he was back as the Cape's counselor. In 1928, he argued a case before the Interstate Commerce Commission in Washington, D.C., supporting the Missouri Pacific Railroad's plan to extend service to Cape Girardeau. At that time, only the Frisco Railroad served the city. The commission agreed to promote competition between the two lines. "We considered that quite a break for the city," Limbaugh said.

Yet it paled in significance to the completion that same year of the long-awaited bridge across the Mississippi River. Prior to that, the only way to get from the Missouri shore to Illinois was by ferry, which seemed to take forever. The bridge became the catalyst for the Cape's development into a regional trading center. The town was, finally, on its way.

Within a year, however, the Depression hit the Cape. "It was one of the saddest times that Cape Girardeau has ever seen," Grandpa Limbaugh, known as "Pop," told the *Missourian*. "People who were engaged in business, they suffered losses and the living conditions declined. The farmers suffered terribly, too." Fortunately, most families in the Cape, because they did not have big investments to lose, such as real estate, survived the 1930s relatively intact, and were able to put their lives back together.

Rush Limbaugh, persistent from birth, just plowed ahead with his impressive legal career, compiling two highly respected reference volumes on Missouri probate law, and became very active in the state Bar Association. He also took his first major step into an arena that has remained a Limbaugh passion for almost seventy years—politics.

In 1918, the Republican Party had asked him to run for mayor, but he was only twenty-seven, three years younger than the minimum requirement, and although he resigned after only a brief tenure as a state representative in 1931–32, which was a part-time job in those days, Rush Limbaugh, Sr., had already set a standard of outspokenness and civic responsibility that is practically a family rite.

Limbaugh left public office to devote more time to his law practice, but he never abandoned public concerns. In 1936, he was a delegate to the Republican National Convention in Cleveland, and served as chairman of the Cape Girardeau County Republican Committee for ten years. In the late 1950s, he taught law classes in India. Today, at 101, he remains the oldest practicing attorney in Missouri, and perhaps the nation.

Limbaugh was also determined to leave behind a large family, and his wife, Bee, was a willing participant in this enterprise. She bore five children, including Rush, Jr., who arrived in 1918. Almost from his youth, Rush, Jr., was a clone of his dad. He, too, went to the University of Missouri Law School, and possessed the same public-speaking talents.

But World War II interrupted his anticipated climb through the legal profession, sending him to the China-Burma-India theater as a flight instructor. As a highly-regarded pilot, he was chosen to fly members of the Chinese Army to their home base at the end of the war, and the squadron he trained was being prepared to attack Japan when the atomic bomb ended hostilities in 1945. He was discharged as a major.

Rush, Jr., never engaged in combat, but the Cape didn't care. He came home a hero, and immediately followed his father's example of civic leadership. In 1946, he and the elder Limbaugh formed a law firm, which represented the college, and he was particularly instrumental in helping his hometown make a smooth transition to peace through the expansion of the local airport, which, as Harris Field, had been operated by the Army during World War II.

As the *Southeast Missourian* noted when Rush Limbaugh, Jr., died in 1990: "A skeptical public had to be convinced of the need for and benefits that might flow from a modern airport. Through years of effort, Rush led so many others who overcame those objections. Old Harris Field became the new airport, complete with a 6,500-foot runway that could land most any aircraft. Cape Girardeau truly entered the 20th Century, in large part because of the efforts of Rush Limbaugh Jr."

The Limbaughs always worked hard but have had another important ally through the years. One might call it Limbaugh Luck. On May 21, 1949, Rush Limbaugh, Jr., married Mildred (Millie) Armstrong in Kennett, about ninety miles from the Cape. While the Limbaughs were welcoming the new member of the family at 4:00 P.M., a funnel cloud was rapidly making its way toward Cape Girardeau. "We saw a terribly ugly-looking cloud a long way away," said Rush, Sr., years later. "It looked like a cloud filled with danger." And it certainly was. When it eventually touched down, it killed twenty-two people, injured hundreds, and caused $4 million in damage.

Just a few minutes after the tornado hit, the rain diminished and all was quiet, as if nothing had happened. But the impact was very real, and would be felt for many years in a town that has had few other big moments in history. Rush Limbaugh, Sr., and his wife returned from the wedding to find the roof of their home stripped off and the second-story walls severely damaged, and yet his family was among the more fortunate. Most of the area had no power or water.

"People said they knew something was going to happen when Rush got married," recalls Millie Limbaugh, "but they said they didn't know all hell was going to break loose." The newlyweds, fresh from their ceremony, spent the first month of their life together sharing an apartment with Rush's suddenly homeless parents. It wasn't the way they had expected to start a marriage.

Mildred Armstrong, eight years younger than her new husband, was the perfect catch for the upstart lawyer. She was bright, attractive, and most important of all, she possessed the humor and humility that would balance her husband's sternness and sanctity. He lived in his mind, always contemplating the future of democracy and patriotism. She lived in her soul, always offering the vote of confidence when things seemed at their most precarious. They met in 1945 at a college dance. He was in uniform. She was in love.

But any marriage possibilities were delayed because Millie had plenty of ambition. She wanted to be a professional singer, and even moved to Chicago to give it a try. She joined a band, but it didn't work out. She moved back to Cape Girardeau and settled in for a long career of taking care of Limbaughs.

The next assignment became official on January 12, 1951. American troops were in Korea, Marilyn was conquering Hollywood, DiMaggio was about to play his last season, and Millie Limbaugh was giving birth.

From the start, there was no doubt what the proud parents would name the seven pound-six ounce boy—Rush Hudson Limbaugh III, out of respect for the new grandpa. And Rusty, as he was called for years by his family and friends, wasted little time claiming his rightful stake in the Limbaugh legacy. "He didn't talk until he was two, and then he never shut up," Millie said. "One day, his father was teaching a Sunday class, and he had Rusty in the car, and Rusty, all of a sudden, said: 'Daddy, who was before God?'"

At two and one-half, Rusty could recognize car models. One night, the family had dinner with the head of a local Ford outlet. "The new cars came out in the *St. Louis Globe Democrat*," Millie said, "and Rusty went down the list and named all of them. It was just phenomenal. The man was just amazed." Millie remembers, however, that Rush did not exhibit model behavior in the classroom. In kindergarten, Rush's teacher told her that if he didn't hurry up and change his ways, he'd never grow up to be the man his grandfather or father had become.

Sometimes, though, it seems Rush Hudson Limbaugh III almost skipped boyhood, or, at least, was extremely bored with the entire process. His brother, David Limbaugh, who followed the family tradition by becoming a lawyer in Cape Girardeau, and has remained Rush's confidant and legal adviser during his remarkable rise to prominence in the last five years, recalls young Rusty's unusual attraction toward adults.

"When my parents' friends came over," said David, who is two years younger, "he always enjoyed talking to them and loved listening to their conversations. He was ahead of his time in terms of maturity."

Millie says that her son's desire to be older lasted far beyond his adolescent years. "Even when he was thirty," she said, "he said, 'I can't wait until I'm forty.' " Many of his high school friends were a year older. "I wanted to be an adult all my life," Rush told the *Sacramento Bee* in 1986. "I hated being a kid. Adults made me feel better about myself. They seemed to be interested in what I had to say. To my peers, I was a dryball, a deadbeat."

That doesn't mean Rusty did manage to skip boyhood, and its natural rendezvous with mischief. Along with his brother David, his most trusting accomplice, and a few close friends, Rusty became a very efficient practitioner of pranks, a skill he perfected in his early radio days. The phone was a popular instrument for this purpose.

In one prank, Rush and his cohorts called to have pizzas delivered to the homes of teachers they didn't like. He and his buddies would then quickly hide around the block to see the disgruntled faces of the teachers, who immediately realized they had been the victims of adolescent humor. On a few occasions, the Limbaugh brothers sent telegrams to Walter Alston, the manager of Rusty's favorite team, the Los Angeles Dodgers, claiming to be someone else and making arrangements to meet him after a game at the clubhouse or hotel. Of course, they never showed up.

Another popular trick was to make up contests over the phone in which people could win prizes.

"Rusty could make his voice sound like an adult," recalled Valle. "People would show up at the hotel dining room at the Optimists Club during lunch looking for their prizes. It made the news a couple of times. I don't think anyone ever got caught." Rusty also picked people out of the phone book and convinced them to play 'Know Your Bible Contest.' "One of the older folks we'd call was Ezra Borntragger," Rush told the *Bee*. "We'd call ten people in all and ask Bible questions and they were never wrong. We'd send a cab to take them to Red Star Baptist Church for their prizes."

Like any normal American boy, Rusty loved baseball. His father often flew the family in the used Cessna 182 he owned to Busch Memorial Stadium in St. Louis to watch the Cardinals play, but somehow Rusty became drawn to the Dodgers, and especially their new speedster, Maury Wills. The family often stayed in the same hotel as the Dodgers. Rusty was so fascinated by how Wills achieved full acceleration on the second step when he stole bases that, in 1960, he began corresponding about five times a season with the Dodger shortstop. Wills answered the letters, and in 1965, they finally met in person when the team came to St. Louis.

The experience was an early lesson in perseverance, and the advantage of making contacts with the rich or famous. Wills also gave Rusty someone else to mimic, which was one of his favorite hobbies. "His [Rush's] image was probably that of a portly guy," Crowe said, "but in reality, anything that guy put his mind to, he could do. He idolized Maury Wills and became a potent base-stealer in Little League."

Crowe and Rusty's other peers also marveled at his ingenuity in the job market. At thirteen, he began working as a shoeshine boy at a barbershop near the college. The work didn't pay well, a couple of bucks an hour, but it gave him another entry into the stimulating adult world that he admired so much.

"He was shining shoes with these adult males who were always carrying on lively political discussions with the barbers and their buddies," Crowe said, which allowed Rusty to "polish his communication skills. This is when the barbershops were packed with people. It was outrageous to us that he had a real job. The rest of us were paperboys or cutting grass."

But his pranks and shoeshine work were mere sideshows to the new main attraction of Rusty Limbaugh's growing obsession. The Golden Age of radio might have already passed into nostalgia—the big status symbol in Cape Girardeau, as everywhere else in America, was owning a television set—but young Rusty was mesmerized by the sound coming from the box without pictures, and that spell has never let go of him.

As a boy, Rush was deeply influenced by two Midwest radio personalities. One was Harry Caray, the popular Cardinals' baseball broadcaster, who could be heard on KMOX-AM in St. Louis. Caray, full of bluster and bombast, taught Rusty how to exaggerate and embellish. By age ten, Rusty could do a perfect Harry Caray and often did the play-by-play of an imaginary Cardinals game in front of family members and friends.

His other hero was Larry Lujack, the offbeat disc jockey from WLS-AM in Chicago, who taught him how to entertain. Lujack was a master of crazy shtick, and years later, was labeled the "Great Cynic of Chicago" by a *Chicago Tribune* reporter. Rusty spent countless hours in his basement room or at his grandfather's house pretending to be a disc jockey. "I'd sit by the window of my house with the walkie-talkie receiver," recalled Crowe, "and he'd be on the CB radio, giving a little banter and then playing a song. He was already pursuing the radio dream in grade school."

Sometimes, Rusty got so carried away with his dreams, he forgot about everyone else. "One day," his mother recalled, "I went down to play some of my music, and all that was on it was rock 'n' roll. He had taped over my reels."

2

STILL, THERE WAS THE MATTER OF ADOLESCENCE
to get through before he could leap into adulthood
and a life in radio. Home was his toughest, and
most important, hurdle.

The Limbaugh family lived on Sunset in a middle-
class Beaver Cleaver neighborhood—white houses
with green shutters and tended lawns, where everyone knew too much about everyone else's business.
Kids flocked over to the house all the time to play
with the pinball machine, and in later years, for
marathon sessions of poker, spades, or crazy eights
in the large basement. "That was our salvation,"
Millie recalled. The teens had their own space.

The rest of the house was dominated by Rusty's
father, who weighed, at his peak, almost four hundred pounds. Propped up like Archie Bunker in
his favorite living room chair, he would tell Rush's
friends to fetch him a soda or popcorn, and then
he'd host the first Rush Limbaugh Show, three decades before his son became a millionaire with the
same idea.

No matter who came over, and a lot of people did,
Limbaugh, with his loud, booming voice, would
rave for hours about the vices of Communism, and

17

the virtues of Democracy and old-fashioned, honest, rugged American individualism. "We would challenge him to get him revved up so he'd talk a lot," recalled Valle. "But you were on shaky ground any time you argued with him. He had a brilliant mind, and liked to argue and debate." Even after Rusty graduated from high school and moved from the Cape, some of his high school cronies still came by frequently to hear the latest world update from Rush, Jr.

He was conservative when it wasn't fashionable, before Ronald Reagan, even before Barry Goldwater became the spiritual leader of the Republican Party's hardliners. Rush, Jr., gave speeches to every group in town he could find. "He loved making speeches more than practicing law," Millie recalled. "He made a speech once about whatever happened to the signers of the Declaration of Independence. He was asked to do it a lot."

Like most right-wingers, Limbaugh believed Communism was contrary to human nature, both in theory and practice, because it was unrealistic to expect people not to strive for excellence. He considered it a monolithic force set on global conquest.

David Limbaugh understood Karl Marx's theory of surplus values in sixth grade, and that knowledge hadn't come from any textbook. "My dad had given a speech about it," recalled David, who tried to apply his new conviction to the classroom. "I remember a math teacher wanted to give everybody equal grades, and I accused him of employing Communism, which it was."

Rush Limbaugh, Jr., didn't reserve his political rantings for the family or close associates. One night, a neighbor called the Limbaugh residence trying to peddle *Time* magazine, which some conservatives felt was too closely aligned with the dreaded leftist agenda. The man of the house wasn't buying.

"My dad lambasted him over the phone," David said, "and said, 'it might as well be printed in Russian. It's equivalent to *Pravda*.' They ended up in a shouting match." Another popular topic at home centered around the growing teenage rebellion of the 1960s. The father, representing the older generation suddenly under siege, was naturally outraged by what was going on in the streets and college campuses of America.

He felt his country was coming apart. Vietnam, and other defining events of that time, such as the trial of the Chicago 7 antiwar activists, according to David Limbaugh, "further entrenched my dad in his conservative convictions, and made him that much more fearful for the future of the country. He believed that we weren't letting the military fight it, and we were letting the politicians run it, and that's why we were in trouble, and the lesson from Vietnam was not that we shouldn't have intervened, but if we made the decision to intervene, we should have gone in and intended to win, as opposed to half-assing it."

His sons paid close attention, absorbing their father's viewpoints almost without a word. From the beginning, there was very little discord in the Limbaugh household. In 1960, when Rusty was only nine, the philosophical and political battlegrounds had already been clearly delineated.

"When Kennedy beat Nixon in 1960," recalled childhood friend James Kinder, "there was a Magic Marker in their [Rusty and David's] upstairs bedroom, and on the wall it was scrawled: *'Kennedy Won. Nixon Lost. Darn.'* " (The boys' father, according to a family friend, always contended that Chicago Mayor Richard Daley had stolen the election for Kennedy, and, years later, that Watergate was pure politics, a trumped-up scandal to embarrass Nixon.)

Four years later, in 1964, at thirteen, Rusty was pro-Goldwater all the way. "Rusty said 'Lyndon Johnson's a crook,' " Crowe said. "He said he was no good and that the country was going to elect him on all this maudlin sentiment on Kennedy being assassinated. When LBJ was elected, Rusty said, 'Look at all these people he's sending to Vietnam, and he said he wasn't going to do it. He's screwing all of you.' "

Neither did Rusty waste time taking his views into the classrooms of Central High School. In Kathryn Sackman's history class, he and his friends defended the United States commitment to South Vietnam, frustrating the much-maligned teacher. "They were pro-escalation," said classmate Janet Ruopp. "They just wanted us to go in there and bomb the heck out of them and get out. One day, she was so frustrated, she touched a globe with her pointer and ended up knocking it out a third-story window. Rusty and his friends were so forceful that the other side never got much of a chance to say anything."

Which is what Rusty and David must have felt listening to dear old Dad harp on his latest liberal victim. But David insists his father, for all the monologues, was always receptive to an exchange of views. "It was not a unilateral discourse, by any means," David said. "There would be give and take and my dad forced my brother and me to think in a discriminating way, and not accept blindly things we would read or hear in the media, and to challenge things that did not square with our human experience." That's a lesson that Rush, never a friend of the Establishment press, continues to apply today.

Friends like Crowe and Valle insist Rusty often sat passively during these discussions, almost afraid to challenge his father's authority. But his brother saw it differently. "One of his greatest attributes," David said, "is that he is a good listener, and literally absorbs everything, and I think what he was doing was sitting around quietly and absorbing knowledge, and though he's reputed to be a loudmouth and always talking, that really wasn't the case."

Rush, too, is fully aware of how those talks shaped his future on radio. "I really consider the greatest education I ever got was from my dad," he said in a 1987 interview with the *Missourian*. ". . . I really think I learned more just from the times that we would sit down and talk and argue than I did in any other way."

Religion also contributed greatly to Rusty's character. As much as his father's relentless political rhetoric framed his son's positions on a host of foreign and domestic issues, religion, equally reinforced by both parents, gave Rusty Limbaugh the underlying code of uncompromising morality that may be even more relevant. "He [Rush, Jr.] just studied religion a great deal," Millie said, "and would love it when the Mormons or other groups came to the door." It was an opportunity for him to lecture *them*.

Rush, Jr., taught Sunday school at Centenary Church, was a choir director, and served as a lay member of the annual Missouri Conference of the United Methodist Church. At home, his religious teachings penetrated even the most secular conversations.

"It [religion] caused us to believe in family values," said David Limbaugh. "My dad used to say morality descends from God, that human beings wouldn't have a moral code if it didn't come from God, and we'd live in a state of anarchy. We don't believe in moral relativism, secular humanism; we believe in God and immutable laws, the primacy of the human species. From that flow a lot of his [Rush's] political views."

As such, the Limbaughs kept things pretty strict at home. Neither parent, when it came to discipline, ever contradicted the other in front of the boys. The message was very clear: Don't ever try to play one parent off the other, because if you cross us, you will pay. Of course, Rush and David, like any youngsters, were curious to see how far the boundaries could be widened and learned the hard way that their parents were firmly in control.

"His father was a no-nonsense disciplinarian," recalled Robert Denton, a friend of Rush's in junior high school. "You were on your best behavior over there . . . I remember being afraid of his father. He was just kind of gruff, so you didn't warm up to him very much. Rusty and him kept their distance. They had moved into a very large house and Rusty's room was downstairs in the basement, and his father, because of his size, didn't move around very much. He kind of just sat in the chair in the living room, and so we stayed away from that area of the house."

The Limbaugh boys, however, discovered there was plenty of support, too. David Limbaugh recalls that his father, even after extremely busy days at the office, found enough time to show interest in his son's activities. "One time, when I first started reading the Hardy Boys books, I was so excited about it that I made him promise to read it one night so I could discuss it with him the next day," David Limbaugh said. "I remember coming and checking on him, and he literally read the whole book, a kid's book. He read it just because I asked him to, and that was a neat thing."

David liked to learn, and was a good student, but Rusty never got much academically out of high school. Sure, there were certain classes that intrigued him and he enjoyed hanging around his clique of friends, but his mind was focused elsewhere.

He was never part of the popular crowd, although he certainly had the necessary credentials. He was bright enough and funny enough and well-connected enough—the Limbaughs were one of the most highly regarded families in town, with plenty of money to command substantial social clout, and his friends' parents were also part of the upper crust. But Rusty was a bit on the chunky side, and didn't have a steady girl, which is one of the age-old prerequisites for membership in the in-crowd—you must be part of "a couple."

He hung out with Valle, Kinder, and Crowe, who were generally perceived as fun-loving intellects, but even as his friends began to discover the opposite sex, Rusty found very little success in that area. "He was interested in girls," Valle said, "and how the rest of us did it. He was a little hesitant to jump into it like the rest of us had." Denton said he remembers that in seventh grade, Rush discovered the birds and the bees. "His parents finally told him," Denton said. "He was amazed. And then he told me about it. I do remember each of us were a little amazed that our parents would do something like that."

A few girls had crushes on him, but Rusty didn't act on them. He never brought girls home for dinner to meet his parents. He did not go to the Prom, and sometimes he was an outright embarrassment. "One time, he went up to the class beauty and said, 'Do you like me?' to her," recalls one high school friend. "She said 'Oh, sure, Rusty.' No one wanted to hurt his feelings, but it was kind of a weird, awkward moment in one's adolescence."

As a freshman and sophomore, despite his general apathy, Rusty followed the typical high school program. He was a member of the debate team and kicked field goals for the Central High Tigers.

But his unbridled passion for radio consumed him, and the clever impersonations in school and the make-believe broadcasts at home with the walkie-talkies and CBs had long outlived their novelty. Adolescent or not, he was ready for a real test.

Fortunately, he had a connection under the same roof. His father was the attorney and one of seven owners of five-thousand-watt KGMO-AM in Cape Girardeau. At sixteen, Rusty asked his father to get him a part-time job at the station. The other owners agreed, and Rush Limbaugh III's radio career officially got underway.

At Central, the show was an instant sensation. For months, except for a few close friends, most of the student body didn't recognize this new, engaging disc jockey—he called himself Rusty Sharpe on the air—spinning their favorite records.

Then, an article in the school paper, the *Tiger*, unmasked his true identity, and Rusty's popularity, among some classmates, at least, soared for the first time. The high schoolers cruised up and down Broadway, with Rusty's voice blaring from the speakers, a youth rebellion in full throttle. "We'd get out of school at 3:00 or 3:30, and the first thing you'd do was get in your car and turn the radio on," Valle said. Rusty had the dream job.

"While we were doing a report for English, he would be doing a report on the musicians," remembered Julia Jorgensen, a classmate who is now a teacher at her alma mater. "He had a story to go along with every song. Even then, he knew when people were born, when they died, who they dated, and how the record came together."

Rusty reveled in his new role, but apparently, it didn't solve all the agony of adolescence. "I loved music, plus I wanted to be popular," he told *Vanity Fair* in 1992, explaining some of his motivation for working at KGMO. "Here I am, playing the music these people like; they can call me and make requests. I can be a source of happiness, a source of satisfaction—*that* will make me popular. It didn't. All it did was make people think that I walked the halls of high school as a stuck-up snob."

Over the years, however, he has consistently acknowledged how his first job in radio might have been the turning point in his life. "If my father hadn't owned a real small portion of KGMO, things might have turned out differently," he told the *Missourian* in 1987. "My father enabled me to learn the radio business and get my own radio show back then. That was luck. I fell into it." If not, perhaps these days, Rush would be filing motions at a Missouri courthouse.

Rusty's work at KGMO suddenly made high school even more irrelevant. There was simply no time for it. He was even working most weekends at the station, and when he wasn't on the air, he spent a lot of time hanging out at the studio with friends, listening to tapes. One song he kept playing over and over was "Suspicious Minds," by Elvis Presley. When at home, he'd tinker some more, editing tapes on his reel-to-reel recorder in his bedroom hideaway. Radio had become his whole reason for existence, and schoolwork became the biggest casualty.

In an interview with the *New York Times*, Limbaugh traced his disinterest in school even further back. "My mother would be fixing me breakfast," he said, "and I'd be listening to the guy on the radio. He'd be having fun, and I was preparing to go to prison." Well, in the late 1960s, at sixteen, too young to vote or shave, he was the one having fun. He was the guy on the radio who made others jealous.

In 1989, when Rush delivered the commencement address at his alma mater, he talked about how little he had attended high school. "It made me angry," Jorgensen recalled. "Not everyone has the brains Rusty has. It bothered me that Rusty came off so arrogant because that isn't the way I remember him."

In the summer between his sophomore and junior years, Rusty convinced his parents to send him to the Elkins Institute of Radio and Technology in Dallas. Because he would sometimes be the only person at KGMO—the station even shut down for a few hours each day—he was required to have the proper broadcasting license.

Six weeks in Dallas would do it. Rusty borrowed the money from his father, who borrowed it from the bank. Millie Limbaugh said her husband later regretted that decision because he felt he had prematurely helped guide Rusty into a future that should have waited, at least until after high school or even college.

"He [Rusty] was thrown in with people [at the station] that his dad was afraid would have him have a warped attitude about life." Rush, Jr., certainly admired his son's work ethic, rare for a teenager in a dawning era of restlessness, but was very concerned that it would force him to stray away from the most important objective of that time in his life—making plans for college. From there, Rusty could apply his mental discipline and become what he was predestined to be, a lawyer.

The Limbaughs also felt their son wasn't taking full advantage of what Central High had to offer. Before he got the job at KGMO, "he was normal," said his mother. "Once he got that license, he divorced everything extracurricular."

But if the Limbaughs were worried about their son's being co-opted by the Movement, forget it. The 1960s, for the most part, only grazed Central High and Rusty Limbaugh. "I played all the protest songs," Rush told *Sacramento Magazine* in 1988. "All those things like John Lennon and the Yoko Ono Band. But I never really listened to the lyrics. Rock to me was never anything special. It's basically all about rebellion and blue jeans. To this day, I have never owned a pair of blue jeans."

The sixties finally did arrive a few years late, in 1972. "Cape Girardeau was on some sort of delay," Crowe said. Except for some nearby black rioting in response to the 1968 assassination of the Rev. Martin Luther King, Jr., there were few hints that America was undergoing a racial and generational upheaval.

Drug use at the school wasn't rampant, and few students made any brash fashion or hair statements; Rusty wore a flattop, which, in itself, was a statement of the status quo. Even the more conventional adolescent vices didn't tempt the square Limbaugh. Not even beer. "I remember him saying, 'Why would anyone want to drink this stuff? It doesn't even taste good,' " Valle recalled. (Two decades later, Rush told his listeners that he has tried marijuana, but he clearly wasn't thrilled with the experience. However, disc jockey Randy Raley said he shared a joint with Rush at a Kansas City party in the late 1970s, and "he seemed to have a good time.")

The Vietnam War, however, could not be so easily brushed aside. However one may have felt about the Johnson administration's motives and the wisdom of fighting a guerrilla war on the enemy's turf, the danger of being drafted—and dying—was very real, and Cape Girardeau, like hundreds of small towns from coast to coast, was going to lose some of its brightest future stars to a battle few wanted to wage.

Yet, for all of his father's patriotism, and deep-rooted fear of Communism, Rusty did not enlist to preserve those ideals. The official explanation, David Limbaugh believes, is that Rush had a student deferment and, like his father, had a pilonidal cyst which qualified him for a medical deferment. "He did not try to actively avoid the draft," insisted David Limbaugh, "and my dad, being the super patriot he was, would not have supported him in that. He would have figuratively murdered him if he had tried that." (In contrast, according to Millie Limbaugh, Rush, Jr., told people he had persuaded authorities to overlook a hearing problem and let him enroll in flight school during World War II.)

Christine Craft, who hosts a nightly talk show for KFBK in Sacramento and got to know Limbaugh in the 1980s, doesn't buy that version. "He was such a hawk on this issue of defending his country," Craft said, "that he got out because of an ingrown hair? That tells me something."

As Rush has become well-known, some people, especially bitter war veterans, have questioned his deferment, and insisted he doesn't have the right to make comments about American military intervention around the globe when, given his opportunity in the 1960s, he had been too cowardly to serve. In 1991, Rush was an outspoken advocate of the United States waging war against Saddam Hussein. Rush's stock reply has been that one doesn't need to be a drug addict to know that taking drugs is not a good idea.

"Like a lot of people in that era, he wanted out, and any way he could find to get out, he did," said Mary Jane Popp, who worked with Rush at KFBK. "I don't think anyone would hold that [against him], but then you don't get on the air and say nasty things about what's happened, or say, 'This is what should have been done.' . . . They [Vietnam vets] were upset. 'You got out because of an ingrown hair?' That bothers people. 'Don't tell us what it was like!' Don't judge people from that era, cause you don't know. You weren't a part of it.'"

But, in response to one irate caller on his show a few years ago, Rush finally decided to give his critics what they always wanted. He boldly admitted that he was too frightened to fight in Vietnam, and that he appealed to his wealthy father to make things right with the draft board. He said his father wrote a $3,000 check which kept him out of the army. Rush's sarcasm didn't work. People bought it. "That made my dad mad," recalled David Limbaugh, "because he thought Rush was gratuitously getting himself in trouble when he didn't need to, because a lot of idiots believed it."

But, for many ex-classmates, the Vietnam War is ancient history. For most of them, now in their early forties, with their own kids in high school, and their memories fading with each birthday, one of the moments that stands out about their former friend-turned-superstar is his role in a Central High film that he and some buddies made during their senior year. Crowe sold the student council on the idea of a melodrama patterned after the popular black-and-white serials in which the girl gets rescued just before she's about to be run over by a train. They called the picture, *You're a Mean Man, Cyanide Barrenheart*, and the star was, of course, Rusty Limbaugh.

Known for his stinging wit, which could be turned against teachers he didn't like without their even realizing it, he was the perfect choice for the villain. It gave him another chance to demonstrate his skills as the consummate entertainer, and he certainly delivered. He could play a great bad guy, a skill that would make him millions twenty years later.

The credits rolled on the screen, and soon, the Class of 1969 at Central High—about 425 students—rolled on to graduation and the rest of their lives.

3

MOST WENT EAGERLY OFF TO COLLEGE, READY TO collect the credentials they would need for the professions that awaited them. Not Rusty. He didn't need any more credentials. He knew he was ready right then to assume his rightful position on the dial. But the most imposing figure in his life was still his father, and he wanted to please the old man just as intensely as he wanted to make it in radio. For much of his life, those two priorities collided head-on, causing friction and frustration for both of them. So, against his better instincts, he postponed his dream and enrolled at Southeast Missouri State.

"He was going to school primarily to placate his father," said Peter Bergerson, his American government instructor and friend. Rusty, after all, had already experienced his first taste of the college grind, and had not found it too appetizing. During his senior year at Central, also to appease the old man, he took Speech 101 at the college. Rush, Jr., was certainly never hesitant about becoming personally involved in his son's academic career.

"His father came to me and said that his son had gotten senioritis, and wasn't challenged much," recalled Bill Stacy, Rusty's speech teacher that semester. "He wondered if I'd let Rush come into my class because, with the talent he had in communication, maybe he'd become kind of intrigued by a college class and he'd get turned on, and that would be the start to the road to law school."

That road, of course, had been sealed off many years earlier, but his father was in no mood to accept the truth, not yet. He kept clinging to the hope that something might straighten his son out, and he was going to do his damnedest to locate that remedy. It wasn't going to be Speech 101, that's for sure. Rusty did not do well, primarily because he neglected to provide detailed outlines of his talks.

But one day, in another moment of chaos, a glimpse of the future peeked out of nowhere. The assignment was fairly routine: Pick a topic and give a speech. When it came to Rusty's turn, the eighteen-year-old was befuddled. His mind was on songs, not speeches, and he hadn't prepared anything. Still, without hesitation, he stood up in front of his classmates and spoke extemporaneously for seven minutes. Stacy doesn't remember the subject. He does remember the response.

"He opened his mouth and out came beautiful words and connected language," Stacy said. "He didn't stumble or stagger or think for a word, and as I looked over the class, their jaws just fell open. He could tell he had people in the palm of his hands."

Once in college full-time, Rusty took speech again. This time, he got a "C," but again, he ignored outlines. He also didn't attend class often enough to take the written exams. The reports of his low attendance in that class and his poor grades in other subjects got back to his parents, who decided it was time to discipline their apathetic son. Enough was enough.

They figured they would strike where it would hurt Rusty the most—his car. Rusty drove a blue Pontiac LeMans, which he worshiped. He had purchased it in high school, borrowing the money from his father, and cruised around town in high style, the grown-up DJ who owned Cape Girardeau.

For two weeks, Millie Limbaugh drove Rusty to class and his job at the radio station, an experience one might consider rather humiliating for a teenager trying to make a respectable impression in the adult world. The punishment, however, did not achieve its purpose. "I suspect he went in one door and out the other," said Millie Limbaugh. "Apparently, he wasn't upset enough."

That didn't stop his father. Two weeks into the semester, Bergerson got a call from the powerful Cape Girardeau attorney. "He wanted to know how his son was doing in class," Bergerson recalled. "I said, 'I don't know. I've got 150 kids, but if he's having some problems, have him come in and see me.' I was surprised at the call, and what surprised me even more was that I had an unlisted number at the time." But the Limbaugh firm had represented the university for years, so no unlisted phone number could remain a secret for very long.

Soon it became apparent that no amount of parental interference, however, could overcome the unpleasant reality: Rush Limbaugh III was not made for college. Once his family had finally let go of the fantasy of bringing another Limbaugh into the

firm, their next approach was to, at least, persuade
him to obtain a university diploma. At least with a
degree, once Rush eventually quit radio, he could
have something to impress potential employers.

Speech class didn't keep Rush interested in college but Mary Puls did. She was his first serious
relationship. They went to movies and shot pool
at Rush's house. "They were hot and heavy for
a while," recalled her sister, Linda Boston. "He
was very good to her." Mary's mother, Doris Puls,
said Rush used to send her daughter long-stemmed
flowers all the time. "Frankly, I don't think she was
too excited about him," said Doris Puls. "He was
more excited about her than she was about him.
She liked him fine. She liked the attention."

Soon, though, the attention wasn't enough, and
Mary was certainly getting enough of it from other
guys, so it was time to say good-bye to Rusty. He
did not take it well. "He was stung by it," Bergerson
said. "He's always had a substantial ego, and what
stung him the most" was that she initiated the
breakup. The sting lasted for some time. Linda
Boston recalled meeting Rush's father after the
breakup. "I said to [Rush, Jr.] 'My sister dated
your son,' and he said, 'Yeah, your sister broke
my son's heart.' He was not too friendly for the
rest of the time."

Finally, in February 1971, with no girl and no
goal at Southeast Missouri State, Rush was offered
a job as a disc jockey for WIXZ-AM in Pittsburgh.
He decided to quit school and leave the womb.
His father, overprotective to the very end, made
one last-ditch effort to hang on to him, but it

was way too late. He would not win this time.

"He sat down and gave me a list of things that would happen as a result," Limbaugh told *Vanity Fair* in 1992. "I would never be able to maintain my social standing. I would never be able to maintain my friends because I'd lose intellectual compatibility. And then he said, 'And you'll never be able to find a decent woman to marry, son. Because what woman wants to marry a man who can't support her?' And I said, 'Well, I don't want to marry a woman like that anyway.' I lied."

His parents were also worried about the precarious nature of the radio business, but they waved their first son good-bye, helped him pack the Pontiac, and wished him luck. It was on to Pittsburgh. "I remember saying, 'Whatever you do, Rusty, be humble and do what your bosses say,' " Millie Limbaugh remembered. But, in the twenty-two years since he left home, humility is the one trait Rush Limbaugh has never learned.

In retrospect, his risky move to quit school at twenty and embark on a career in such an unstable profession as radio was inevitable for an independent soul like Rusty. In a sense, it was a courageous act of rebellion, defying everything his father and grandfather had built for the family in Cape Girardeau. He was rejecting their world, and, by implication, he was rejecting them, and that hurt them greatly.

But, on the other hand, he was also abiding by the fierce individualism that characterized much of their conservative teaching. Rush, Jr., taught his son to think for himself, and that's exactly what he was doing. "He walked to his own drummer," Stacy said, "even in those days. He invented his own rhetoric, rather than read it in a book or try to follow what somebody else had done."

His performance in speech class was the perfect example. "He looked out over that class and saw the people in rapt attention, listening to every word he said," Stacy recalled, "and then, he heard some teacher say, 'You get a 'D' because that didn't work,' and, in his own mind, he's got to be saying, 'Teacher, look at those people looking at me. You're crazy.' "

But the decision, while Limbaugh has never regretted it, also burdened him with a lifelong need to prove himself, to prove that even without a college education and the unqualified blessing of his family, he could make a solid contribution to society and earn enough money to gain their respect.

Even when he began to achieve almost unparalleled success in his business, that fear and uncertainty—have I really done enough?—reasserted itself, robbing him of some of the satisfaction he richly deserved. "He was a part of a very well turned-out family of high achievers," said a radio colleague from the 1980s, "and might have been looked upon as the one who wasn't going to do well. He had a desire for stardom like nothing I've ever seen. I've seen a lot of ambitious people, but never seen anyone want it so bad."

His brother thinks that the constant need for affirmation has been a "big part of his success." Even

Rush, in an 1986 interview with the *Sacramento Bee*, admitted: "I don't have formal recognition that I'm educated and I'm going to prove it over time without a degree. I just read Karl Marx for the first time and plan to get a set of encyclopedias. I read all the time. I want my strength to be my intelligence." Two years later, he elaborated: "The thing that drives me is that I have no college degree. My friends stayed [in college] and got their degrees and didn't have to demonstrate they were intelligent. I realized I had to demonstrate it. I became consumed by newspapers. If I stop reading newspapers, I'm in trouble in this business." Everything in his life was framed by: I'll show 'em all.

First things first, and Pittsburgh was the opening stop on his journey for recognition. He started with the morning shift at WIXZ, a Top 40 station owned by the same executives who ran the popular WIXY in Cleveland, Ohio.

WIXZ, however, suffered from a slight inferiority complex. Although its signal could be heard all over Allegheny County, the jocks broadcast from a small studio in suburban McKeesport. You were in Pittsburgh, and yet you really weren't. The station even installed some offices in a downtown highrise to boost its self-image, which was the same challenge awaiting the raw, twenty-year-old new jock from halfway across the country. But it was the perfect station for disc jockeys like Rush trying to fill a résumé.

He called himself Jeff Christie, and immediately started to carve out his unique identity. Rick Toretti, who wrote the news during Rush's morning shift, arrived shortly before 6:00 A.M. every day, and found the kid had beaten him to the studio, and was already reading every newspaper he could find.

Rush had an opinion about everything, and even though his responsibilities officially confined him to flipping records and giving brief song introductions, he couldn't resist mixing in slices of daily commentary and pet peeves.

Rush Limbaugh, or Jeff Christie, or whatever he called himself, was never going to conform to the boundaries of radio, regardless of its risks. If conformity were going to be his calling in life, he would have attended the University of Missouri Law School, made babies in the Cape, and forgotten about some silly endeavor called radio. "He was on Cloud Nine," his mother recalled about Rush's early days in Pittsburgh. Once, when Rush came back to the Cape for the annual New Year's Day gathering with the Kinders, he was greeted as the victorious hometown boy who had made it out in the real world. "He was the only non–college student there, which was interesting," remembered Crowe. "He drew a crowd, regaling everyone with stories of what he was doing and what Pittsburgh was like."

At WIXZ, Rush reprised his role as the prankster. This time, the pranks were more civilized than the calls he had made as an adolescent in the basement, but the basic thrust was the same. Toretti remembers when Rush called up baseball bat dealers to tell them he was searching for a left-handed bat. He told them he had broken the last one he owned. "They said there was no difference," Toretti said, "and he said, 'Oh, yeah, the big end is on the opposite end.' "

Another time, he called a department store and told the manager he wanted to return a tie he had purchased as a gift. "They weren't too happy about that, and he said, 'Well there's really nothing wrong with it, although I did get some blood on it.' They said, 'You can't return damaged merchandise,' and he said, 'Oh, it's not really damaged. You can't tell there was blood. I snipped it out.' "

Once, he visited the lingerie shop at a local department store, spotted a sales clerk, and went back to the station to call her on the air. He said he was representing AT&T, and was using an experimental picture phone. Rush then went on to describe exactly what the girl was wearing—he had an informer relaying information to him from a nearby store phone—and told her he needed to buy his wife some lingerie. The clerk held the lingerie to the phone, and, naturally, Rush described it accurately. The girl started to go nuts.

Yet, to most of his colleagues, despite his limited experience, he was a pure professional. "He was one of the most cooperative jocks I ever worked with," said Mary Jane Wolf, who handled things in the control room. "I'd give him a whole stack of commercials. All the other guys would gripe, but he'd just go in the production studio, close the door, and crank them out for me with no hassle, always done on time."

From Rush's poise and maturity, notwithstanding the childish phone games, Wolf, like everyone else, assumed that he was much older than twenty "because he knew what he was talking about. He was into world affairs and politics."

He was also into food—again. For Limbaugh, the weight problem has always been a recurring subplot in the background of all the other dramas of his up-and-down careers as a disc jockey and husband. From elementary school through the Excellence in Broadcasting Network, he has flip-flopped between controlling his fat with the latest can't-miss diet, and surrendering to his desires and ballooning back to his original obese form.

In Pittsburgh, the station manager, according to Wolf, made him a bet, promising to spring for a new wardrobe if he lost sixty pounds. Rush, never one to reject a challenge, especially with money and pride on the line, went on a crash diet for six weeks. He ate nothing but vitamin pills and grapefruit juice. He lost weight and won a wardrobe. "The day that he won the bet," Wolf said, "he went out and bought a steak dinner. He said he ate three little bites and couldn't eat anymore cause he was stuffed. Unfortunately, he turned around and gained all the weight back."

Off the air, Limbaugh was the same old square from Cape Girardeau, Missouri. This was 1972, and he was still living in 1952. He liked Ike, not McGovern. Jim Quinn, a highly respected DJ in the Steel City, said the kid stood out from the start. "I was a leaping, screaming, Vietnam War–protesting, long-haired, maggot-infested, dope-smoking jock," Quinn said. "He was not."

Wolf remembers going to a party with Rush that soon deteriorated into a typical 1970s potfest. Wolf became very agitated. Soon the highly exalted joint would be passed to her, and what would she do? Take a hit, and violate her principles? Or quickly pass the marijuana forward and incur the startled frowns of disapproval from her more hip peers?

Then came Rush to save the maiden. "He said, 'You sit here and scratch my back,'" recalled Wolf. "'That way, I'll just take the joint and pass it. Nobody's going to notice, and nobody's going to dare say anything to me. I'm not going to use, and I don't think you have to use it.'" The strategy worked, and Wolf was spared her dilemma. "I was always grateful to him," she said, "that he had enough guts to not take the pot and to shield me from the criticism of those other people."

Sharyn Fialla, an engineer who worked with Rush, found him to be a refreshing change from the traditional overly aggressive male in radio.

"I never felt any pressure from him," said Fialla. "I appreciated that because I was in a situation where everyone was either dealing with me as a threat—someone who might take their jobs—or as a sex object, finally something interesting to look at in the control room. He just dealt with me as a person. My conversations with him weren't centered around, 'What do you want in a relationship?' We talked about deeper, more philosophical things."

But WIXZ's management wasn't exactly buying the new kid's on-air antics, and told him to tone things down. This is a radio station. We play records, not games. Toretti, who established a college station at the Penn State University branch in McKeesport, asked Rush one afternoon to give his students a pep talk about the business. Instead, it resembled a farewell speech.

"He told everyone in the group he was either going to get fired or he was going to quit," Toretti said. "He said they told him to 'play music, give the time, temperature, weather, and that's it.' " His fear was justifiable. Everyone at WIXZ was worried about being fired. "It was a revolving door policy back then," Toretti added. "If you made one mistake, you were gone."

Weeks later, Rush was gone. He had been at WIXZ less than two years. But, anticipating that moment, he had been busy circulating his résumé around town, and it paid off when his work caught the attention of Bob Harper, program director of Pittsburgh's KQV. Harper hired Rush for the evening shift.

"The thing I liked about him the most was that he got the joke of format radio," Harper said. "He knew in his heart that it was funny, that we had disc jockeys who could talk at certain times, jingles that had to be played at certain times, and that a certain kind of record had to follow a certain situation. He could show the fact that this was funny, and he could communicate that on the air."

In those days, politics was not a big part of his radio persona. Off the air, he was clearly opinionated about everything, and would not back away from an argument with anyone who dared to challenge his fundamentally conservative views. "When you called him at home," said Ken Brakewell, another Pittsburgh disc jockey, "you had to listen to minute-long diatribes telling everyone how terrible the American Medical Association was before you could leave a message." On the air, he mostly stuck to music.

Rush was also very competitive, especially in sports. "We were playing a charity softball game before a Pittsburgh Pirate game," said one former disc jockey, "at Three Rivers Stadium. We were playing the Pittsburgh Pirates' wives. He was catching and he put a tag on one of the Pirate wives trying to score, like he was playing in the World Series. This was supposed to be fun."

He was unpolished and undisciplined at KQV, but the talent was undeniable. "You knew he was going somewhere," Brakewell said. He certainly was, and fast—the unemployment line. In 1974, KQV general manager John Gibbs reportedly made the decision to let Rush go. "He [Gibbs] is the guy who told Rush he'd never make it in radio," said Quinn. "He said his best bet was to look toward a sales job." Here, too, it seems Limbaugh could have saved his job if he had been more willing to be a team player, but he obviously concluded the price—his dignity and self-respect—would have been even steeper.

"My general feeling was that he knew what he was doing," said David Limbaugh, presenting a theory that could apply to all of Rush's firings. "He refused to compromise his professional standards for the sake of conforming to what his bosses wanted him to do. He probably knew the results were he'd get fired, but, nonetheless, he chose to do it. He knew he would bounce back, that he was talented, that if he were given a chance, he'd prove it."

Jim Carnegie, who had become KQV's program director, wanted to give him that opportunity, but said Gibbs was adamant about dismissing Rush. "When your boss tells you to do something, what are you going to do?" Carnegie said. "He [Limbaugh] took the firing like a man, that radio is radio. He went back to Cape Girardeau with no bitterness." If not bitter, Rush was certainly bummed out. Suddenly, after a few years as the local boy who made good in the tough, cruel world, he was the local boy back living with his folks, the ultimate disgrace.

He was no longer innocent, and while his high school classmates had graduated from college and were well on their way toward high-paying, prestigious professions, he was in limbo, wondering when, or if, he'd put the headphones on again and become Jeff Christie. The days of pretending to be Harry Caray and Larry Lujack and broadcasting from his safe basement hideaway were long gone.

Radio, as he had painfully discovered, was more than a Missouri teenager's fantasy. It was a job, and often one that didn't last.

4

FOR MONTHS, RUSH SAT AROUND THE HOUSE WITH nothing to do. His mother remembers little about her son's daily agenda, except that "he was bored to death." She felt sorry for him. "He felt like he let himself down and us, too," she remembers.

Still, undaunted by his first two failures in Pittsburgh, Rush sent out résumés and called up contacts at stations across the country, yearning for the opportunity to try again. Radio is, after all, a small fraternity whose members shuttle from station to station like a tribe of gypsies, rarely reaching a final destination, fortunate to find even temporary shelter. Harper, who hired him at KQV, was working in Buffalo when he received Rush's urgent call. "We had solid air staff at the time," said Harper, "and I couldn't hire Rush."

But, mercifully, Jim Carnegie could. As the operations manager for KUDL in Kansas City, he called one day to rescue Rush. For Carnegie, it was a great chance to make up for being forced to fire Rush in Pittsburgh. Millie Limbaugh answered the phone, Carnegie recalled, "and I said, 'Is Jeff Christie there?' And she yelled, 'Rusty, it's for you!' He got on the phone, and said he had no job offers yet. He was in Kansas City within twenty-four hours."

At KUDL, Rush was handed his first opportunity to do what he has always done best—talk. The station was ready to provide more news in its regular programming, and had an opening in its midday shift. "He had kind of a provocative way and was not afraid to take somebody on," said Sandy Martin, the station manager, who became a good friend, "and we really kind of wanted to create that kind of a radio station. We wanted to ruffle some feathers."

Rush loved to ruffle feathers, and although it was not the precise talk show format he became accustomed to later in his career, at least it wasn't more of just flipping records and tossing out obscure music trivia to a gang of infantile teenagers.

By taking some phone calls on the air, he was allowed, for the first time, to reveal his personality and philosophy between songs, and chat with his favorite group—adults. But even Carnegie knew he had to establish limits or else Rush would create his own, and they would most likely go too far for management. "I said, 'Piss them off enough, but don't be too obnoxious,' " he said. " 'Don't go too far left and don't go too far right.' And he did it like a pro. He would pick topics, and piss people off, and they laughed. They loved it."

The show became known as the "gripe line," in which Rush and his loyal listeners complained about the latest example of government inefficiency, from the White House to City Hall.

"One of his kicks was the oil cartel issue," Martin recalled. "He said how bad it was, and that the people didn't understand, and we were just selling our country out." He also complained about the potholes in Kansas City, and the ill-conceived roster moves by the local sports teams. Rush could gripe about anything.

Once again, he became the station's token rightwinger. Most of the disc jockeys were "free-spirited hippies," recalled Jerry Jones, who was one of them, while Limbaugh was perceived as the "extremely conservative guy . . . and we all kind of just chuckled about him. 'Man, what's *his* story? Who's the Nazi kid?' Rush was the station joke at the time."

Jones said Rush's passion for politics wasn't confined to the microphone. "He'd grab anyone that would let him and buttonhole them in the hall," Jones said. "Once you got him started, it was hard to make him shut up. I recall chiding him, 'Hey, Rush, what are you talking about? Why don't you read the papers?' He'd always have a comeback. Whether it was accurate or not was another thing."

But Rush had more to worry about than accuracy in his duels against the liberals at KUDL. Once again, on the air, as in Pittsburgh, he was crossing the boundaries; this was 1975, and talk radio was still not in vogue. "He was a square peg in a round hole," said Lynn Higbee, a KUDL colleague. "The philosophy of the gripe line was to give people a forum to let out steam, but Rush would get involved in the discussions, as well, and then it got away from the music. And if you're a music station, you have to play music, and you can't be talking all the time. He'd overtalk."

Naturally, Rush did not react positively to the station's efforts to keep him under control. "He was like most disc jockeys," Higbee said. "They're never happy being forced into somebody else's mold. He wanted more freedom." Rush was also not the most polite radio personality ever to hit Kansas City. His act was very raw and abusive in those days. He hung up on listeners and called them stupid. He played songs he hated, and explained his reasons to the listeners. His behavior made life difficult for the KUDL management.

On the one hand, the brash disc jockey executed the game plan perfectly, generating tons of listener feedback and good ratings. But, conversely, a few advertisers in this mostly prudish Midwest town became increasingly distressed with Limbaugh's often irresponsible tirades, and even threatened to pull their spots if he didn't back off.

For a station with a weak signal that depended on every dollar, this meant restraining Rush was imperative. Martin and Carnegie took on that job, and it was never easy. "He was told on a number of occasions to keep his opinion to himself," Martin recalled, "and sometimes he would abide by that, and get off the topic. But he's a passionate person and if he got on an issue, he'd stay on it until he was through. He would not go back and play music and cork his opinion."

Carnegie confronted him directly, which normally wasn't the most practical way to handle Limbaugh. Martin employed a softer approach. "You go out with him, have some beers, and get him to a point where he had to listen," she said, "and somewhere along the line, there'd be a compromise, and he'd be okay."

Rush, still in his twenties, was consumed by his work. When he and KUDL general manager Doc Fiddler went to the bar, the talk was, according to Martin, "either work-related or all sports. He really didn't like to philosophize about life or chitchat." Rush was preoccupied with achieving enough to appease the old man in Cape Girardeau. "His father was a real issue with him," she added. "They didn't have a close relationship. His father made him feel like an unaccomplished person and I don't think he felt any worth in broadcasting. He pictured him as a dropout, a flunkie, and really wasn't doing anything for society, or for business. He really could have pulled his own with his father in terms of conversation and argument, but I don't think he ever felt quite satisfied that he came up to par in his father's eyes."

5

ANOTHER REASON RUSH POURED SO MUCH TIME IN-
to his work was because there was nothing else to do;
his romantic life after Mary Puls dumped him was
a complete dud. Not that he didn't try to change
his image. He went on yet another diet, and looked
more attractive, and, in fact, was so proud of the
new, improved Rush Limbaugh that he carried a
photo in his wallet of his more portly days and
showed it to everyone. But he still lacked the confidence to relate easily to women, and assumed he
was fated to stay a bachelor forever.

"He absolutely figured he was going to be a solo
kind of guy," Martin said, "and that was basically
because he wasn't willing to compromise on any of
his attitudes or his habits, and if he wasn't going
to, he didn't expect anybody else would, either. So
he probably would date, and maybe see somebody
until they got sick of each other, and that was it."
He briefly dated Lynn Higbee's daughter, Christi.
But her mother, Jan, said the relationship didn't
go anywhere because of a fundamental philosophical difference in their view of women. "She was
very much into the feminist thing," Jan Higbee
said, "and he was too much of, 'Women, barefoot,

pregnant,' type. She finally couldn't take it any longer."

One day, the perennial bachelor met his first real love. Her name was Roxy Maxine McNeely, and she worked at WHB's radio station sales department. They met through a mutual friend. For Rush, all of his preconceptions about lifetime solitude were instantly transformed by these strange new emotions, which he had always imagined were reserved for more attractive and fortunate men. "He fell madly in love with her," Sandy Martin said, and "really didn't expect to be swept off of his feet. Roxy was very attractive, with long blond hair, and a real sweet gal . . . He was kind of madly in love [with the fact] that he could be madly in love. He just couldn't believe the kinds of feelings he was going through."

His roommate, Bryan Burns, said Rush soon spent the majority of his free time with Roxy, and things got hot and heavy so quickly that the lovebirds decided to move into their own place. But Burns said Rush lived up to his original lease commitment and paid his monthly share of the rent even while staying somewhere else.

Rush's relationship with Roxy, he assumed, would earn him new points of credibility with his family. When Rush spurned college for the first radio gig in Pittsburgh, his dad had warned him he would have trouble finding a woman because his questionable ability as a provider would turn off many prospective candidates. But not in this case. *'See, Dad, you were wrong. I can find somebody!'* Martin recalled that their relationship appeared quite normal. "I remember them being very nice to each other, not overtly loving, but very nice and very attentive to each other," she said. "I don't remember Roxy talking very much, but that's always hard with Rush."

Rush's high school classmate, Craig Valle, and his wife, Beverly, spent a weekend with the new couple fairly early in their relationship, and came away unimpressed with his friend's catch. "She sometimes seemed too cheerful," Valle recalled, "maybe like she was putting on an act. People liked her, but because it was a pretty fast courtship, we really didn't know too much about her . . . maybe she tried too hard."

Just a few months later, on September 24, 1977, Rush and Roxie got married at the Centenary United Methodist Church in Cape Girardeau. The affair brought together the town's pillars in politics and business, a wonderful symbol of the new status Rush Hudson Limbaugh III thought he had finally attained before his family and peers. Roxy was radiant in a gown made of satin and organza with lace and pearls encircling the high neckline. She carried a bouquet of pink roses and miniature white gladiolas. Rush was beaming in his tuxedo. A reception was held at the church social hall following the wedding.

But, within months, there was another gripe line in Rush Limbaugh's life—the one between him and his wife. Rush told *Time* magazine in 1992 that his marriage to Roxy was for the wrong reasons, and other family members and friends contend Rush, twenty-six, was not ready to get married. "I was doing what I thought I had to do," he told *Time*.

"There was romance in the idea of *being* married." Clearly, to Rush, the concept of *being* married was far more important than the tough responsibilities of the marriage itself.

Martin, who was maid of honor at the wedding, says Rush and Roxy's marriage didn't last because each had dramatically opposing expectations of what the institution was all about. She recalled a conversation with Rush that made it apparent he expected his marriage to Roxy to resemble the relationship his parents had built. What he failed to grasp was that this was a much different generation.

"His father was so dominant that he [Rush] just didn't understand why that couldn't happen," Martin said. "He didn't understand a 1970s kind of a woman, somebody with independence, because Jeff [Rush's on-air name] was pretty traditional . . . he probably had convinced himself so well that he wasn't ever going to have that [a wife] that he really didn't have a correct point of view of what a marriage was."

Another problem, according to Martin, was that Roxy realized that Rush wasn't the fathering type, either. "I think Roxy wanted to have a family, and I don't think Jeff wanted to have a family, and I think Jeff's impetuousness and his style kind of got to her, and it just kind of deteriorated," she said. "I don't remember any huge fight . . . It just wasn't what they anticipated, and it just eroded, and it was more work than either one wanted to put into it."

Some who knew the couple well speculate there may have been other reasons for their breakup, such as money. A few family members were concerned that she might be a gold digger. "She acted like she adored him," said one member who wanted to remain anonymous, "but I think she thought [the Limbaughs] were monied people. Others sensed the money thing, too." Roxy, for her part, does not want to talk about her life with Rush. "That's pretty much irrelevant now," she said, refusing numerous requests to be interviewed for this book. Her name now is Roxy Baker, wife of Sgt. Gary Baker, a Missouri Highway Patrol public information officer, who she married in 1981. Her life is quiet.

Whatever caused their divorce, Rush was deeply hurt by the whole experience. To his family, as usual, he remained the same upbeat, unaffected Rusty, never allowing too much vulnerability to penetrate that veneer of strength. But to friends, as much as he tried to manage his emotions there, too, he couldn't put up the same brave front. "He said, 'That's it, I'm through with women. I'm going to be asexual,' " Martin said. "I remember him throwing that out one time, and I said, 'Jeff, I don't think anyone is asexual. They may decide not to participate, but you might check with your doctor.' "

His days at KUDL were also coming to an end. The station, on the market for several years, was finally sold to a Christian broadcasting network in the late 1970s, which meant that there would be no more gripe line and no more Jeff Christie. Radio once again had proven to be just as precarious as his parents had predicted. He had no woman and no work.

Martin said Rush was offered a position with the new company's FM station, but turned it down because it would mean a step backward to flipping records again. Bolstered by the early success of his first legitimate experience in the world of talk radio, even if it wasn't exactly the format he would have preferred, Rush was more determined than ever to conquer his field. There were, after all, thousands of other radio stations across the country, and he was still a very young man.

For instance, across town, there was KFIX-FM, an adult contemporary station in Kansas City. Rush was hired to host a talk show from 7:00 to 11:00 P.M. "He seemed to be a bright guy and have some intensity in him," recalled Jim Gallant, the program director who hired him. "It was worth a shot to see if he could pull in some numbers because he was the type of guy people might listen to and get involved with."

Once again, however, almost immediately, the abrasiveness which got him into trouble at KUDL resurfaced, causing tensions between Rush and station owner Joe Abernathy. "He was just a little too crude," Abernathy said. "He hung up on people if they didn't agree with him. He wasn't able to do what we felt we needed done." Gallant said he warned Rush to cool his act to avoid being fired, but "he wanted to do what he wanted to do." Limbaugh was stubborn again, and soon he was unemployed again, as well.

Finally, the frustration of failure after failure, of the arrogant, power-hungry program directors and station managers having the audacity to believe they actually knew more about radio and entertainment than he did, had reached its threshold.

"I was disillusioned with radio," he told the *Bee* in 1986. "It isn't the real world if that's all you do. Most radio stations are toilets. Some have flushers, some don't. Radio people are a little weird. You're in a little world with a microphone and you have to tell yourself that thousands of people are reacting to you. You go to lunch and nobody knows you. You live a lie in that little room."

6

RUSH WAS READY FOR A HIATUS FROM RADIO, PER-
haps even a permanent career switch, and fortunately, his ex-roommate, Bryan Burns, volunteered
to provide the escape hatch. Burns was the marketing director for the Kansas City Royals. He originally became friendly with Rush through the standard
promotional work he did with local radio stations,
and knew Rush would be a perfect addition to the
front office.

Rush was a huge baseball fan, and the consummate salesman—his ex–Pittsburgh boss was right
about that. But this was certainly not Rush's idea
of a dream job. "I didn't want to do it [work for the
Royals]," Rush said in an interview on sportscaster
Bob Costas's national radio show. "I wanted to
stay a fan. I was never attracted by the glamour
of working at a ballpark, but I decided to do it
because I thought it was time to get serious about
life, which I didn't think broadcasting was."

The task was straightforward: Rush would help
sell the Royals to the fans of Missouri and Kansas.
With his expertise in radio, he was the logical
choice to select tunes for the appropriate moments
to go out over the public address system. He also

helped coordinate special evenings at the stadium for groups from all over the region.

He started in February of 1979, and for a while, to his surprise, Rush seemed to relish this career change.

No more directives from insecure station managers.

No more skittery advertisers threatening to pull their latest spots because of Rush's politics.

No more waiting and wondering when he would be fired next, and how he would scramble to find the next paycheck.

And no more anguished concerns from his father about the family's ultimate underachiever. "I quit radio," he admitted to *Success* magazine, "partly to please my father."

The position with the Royals was, at long last, his first solid move toward security, and his family was hopeful that his decade-long, naive infatuation with radio might give way to sound mature reasoning in a man rapidly approaching his thirties.

"I'm sure I was happy about it," said David Limbaugh. "I always thought there was too much egoism and egotism in the [radio] industry. Based on talking to him, I felt like he would be better off pursuing a job that wasn't in that field." David said the family was happy to see Rush pursue "something that might be more conventional." Even Rush, years later in an interview with the *Bee*, talked candidly about the compromise he had made. "I was willing to sublimate my ego for some security," he said. "Being around the Royals allowed me to meet people I wouldn't have, like the president of Coors."

Many of his peers became jealous of Rush all over again, just as in the old days, when he had been Rusty Sharpe on KGMO in Cape Girardeau. "Once again, he had this primo job," said classmate Julia Jorgensen.

Here he was, the guy who had corresponded with Maury Wills and had impersonated Harry Caray, living out a childhood fantasy by hobnobbing with the likes of George Brett, Willie Wilson, Frank White, and Dan Quisenberry. What more could a grown boy ask for? "When he got fired again from the radio station," Valle said, "and he decided, 'Maybe they're right. Maybe this is not what I should be doing,' everybody thought that it [the Royals job] would be a great job for him to have. There'd be some prestige to being around baseball players."

For the most part, he did a very competent job in his tenure with the Royals. "He was so quick," remembered one colleague. "He had a data bank in his head of music. He always knew which songs to go with in which situations." Essentially, he ran the scoreboard, which was almost like running a radio station.

There was one evening, however, that he will always remember. That's when a group of several thousand came to the ballpark from Olathe, Kansas; it was the night of the year for the folks from this small community.

Rush prepared every detail, and the excitement gradually built up to the highlight of the evening, the first-ball ceremony, when a lucky citizen would have the privilege of tossing the baseball to Royals catcher Jamie Quirk. The big moment arrived, and everything seemed to be in order. Everything, that is, except the baseball. Rush had forgotten to get it. He quickly hollered to the dugout for a ball, and all the players grabbed one and threw them out onto the field. Everyone laughed in his hour of embarrassment. Rush was a popular fellow.

He also established a great rapport with the heavy corporate hitters in town. He may not have followed the Limbaugh tradition of joining the professional ranks and making contacts with all the right business leaders, as Dad and Grandpa had, but he certainly inherited their skills in this department.

From his days with the Royals to his radio job in Sacramento, which resurrected his career, to his current nationwide status as icon, Rush has become a natural in ingratiating himself with the people in power, the people who have money, the people who run America. Now he's one of them.

Away from the office, however, Rush was still suffering the pain of Roxy's departure. "He was very sure of his job," recalled Louise Adams, his secretary with the Royals and surrogate mother, "but he was insecure in his personal life. You know how some people get when a marriage is broken up." Adams said Rush was resigned to the divorce, realizing it "was all for the best, but it wasn't something he was pleased with." She said Rush didn't date for a while after the divorce—maybe Sandy Martin was wrong about him. Maybe Rush would be asexual for the rest of his life.

Instead, again, just as he had during his radio days, he found a release by pouring most of his time and energy into his work, and he got along with everyone, not just the high-level corporate types in the front office. "He knew a lot of people in different walks of life," said Dennis Cryder, who replaced Burns as director of marketing and broadcasting, "may it be an usher or parker or police officer or executive."

It was impossible to miss hearing about all of Rush's friends. "I don't think there was such a thing as a confidential telephone conversation with him because of his pipes," Cryder said. "We had an open office setting with partitions and dividers, and so the booming voice of Rush could be heard through the entire fifth floor."

Rush, still trying to compensate for a lost education, read incessantly, devouring information almost faster than it could be processed. Just because he wasn't in radio anymore didn't mean he had abandoned interest in the rest of the world. "*The Sporting News, Sport Magazine, Newsweek*, the *Wall Street Journal*—they would all be on his desk," recalled Cryder. "He'd consume each and every one of those publications and that night, at dinner in the Press Club, if you wanted to talk about the situation in South Africa or Roger Clemens's Earned Run Average, you could talk about either one of those in great detail with Rush."

But the *Wall Street Journal* could not escort Rush to dinner or hold his hand while he dumped his frustrations over not living up to his parents' high expectations. The scars with Roxy had begun to heal, and Rush was getting restless for new female companionship.

Just at that time, he began to notice a young usherette at the park named Michelle Sixta. He waved to her from a distance, but he was still the shy kid from Cape Girardeau who didn't quite know how to make the first move. Plus their first encounter had not been too cordial.

Encouraged by her boss that she might find Rush very interesting, Michelle bravely introduced herself to him one day at the park. Things didn't exactly click; it was more like Loathe at First Sight. "I happened to run into him coming down the stairwell," Michelle recalled. "He claims I interrupted him while he was having a conversation. My side is that he wasn't talking to anybody, and I introduced myself to him, and he didn't have the time of day for me. So I told my boss I thought he was kind of snobby."

Word quickly got back to Rush about how Michelle felt, and at the next game, he apologized to her. After that, they ran into each other quite frequently, which was no coincidence, and Michelle kept hoping that Rush would ask her for a date. But soon the 1981 baseball season was over, and Rush still hadn't summoned the courage. Michelle went back to college. Rush went back to loneliness.

"I figured, *c'est la vie*. He'll forget about me next season," Michelle said. "I figured there was no way I was going to see him again. He never asked for my number. Maybe he felt I wasn't showing enough interest."

For months afterwards, Rush, as a favor to Louise Adams, phoned her daughter, Suzy, at Central Missouri State University in Warrensburg to see how college life was treating her.

He didn't call for that reason alone. Suzy lived in the same suite as Michelle, and Rush made sure always to pass a message to her. It was obvious to Michelle that Rush was interested in her, but again, nothing happened. Rush was busy in Kansas City; Michelle was focused on college.

Finally, though, in January of 1982, a perfect opportunity came for Rush to go out with Michelle and yet avoid the pressure and expectations of a first date.

He was scheduled to deliver his typical speech promoting the Royals to a gathering in Sedalia, only twenty-five miles from Warrensburg. So he asked Louise Adams to see if her daughter might be interested in joining him. Adams called Suzy, who said she'd love to go. Then, the next day, Rush revealed his true intentions. "He said, 'Do you think Suzy's suitemate, Michelle, would like to go?'" Louise Adams recalled. Adams, the matchmaker of the moment, made the call, and set up the evening. Once in the car, Rush went right after his target, who sat in the middle of the front seat. "I felt like a third spoke the whole evening," Suzy told her mother.

After the speech, the three went out for a bite to eat, and Michelle found him to be surprisingly charming and endearing. She was suffering a bad cold that night, and went to the bathroom with an embarrassing coughing fit. Rush came to her aid with some NyQuil. "He was watching out for me," Michelle said.

A few weeks later, they went on their first official date. Rush took her to Stroud's, one of his favorite Kansas City restaurants, known for its pan-fried chicken and lively atmosphere. The place, a hangout for some of the Royals players, had a lot of charm, with crooked floors and windows. Rush picked her up promptly at eight, and was immediately told he'd have to bring her back by eleven, hardly a long evening for a man anxious to make a good impression. "He was really upset," she recalled. "He felt that it might be an indication of how much interest I had."

But Michelle had plenty of interest. Soon, they became an item, although it made little sense. Michelle was a college student, ten years younger than Rush. Michelle was into art; Rush was into television. Michelle minored in French; Rush minored in the Pittsburgh Steelers. Michelle was interested in exploring the outdoors; Rush was interested in exploring the couch and the computer.

Yet the chemistry between them was evident to everyone. "I think he was more crazy about her than he was about Roxy," said Millie Limbaugh. "He was swept off his feet." Michelle was equally smitten. "I was impressed by the fact that someone that much older with the position he had in the front office would be concerned about what I thought," she said, recalling how he quickly apologized for their initial misunderstanding. She also liked his personality. "I actually could have an intelligent conversation with him," she said.

On April 4, 1982, for her twenty-first birthday, less than two months after they had begun dating, Rush gave Michelle a present she would never forget. He flew her to Dallas for the night, put her up at the Fairmont Hotel, and treated her to an expensive meal. Michelle said Rush did that because "nobody did anything for his twenty-first birthday and he thought that was terrible . . . he wanted mine to be really special."

When Michelle spent a month at the University of Dijon in France during the summer of 1982, Rush stayed in Kansas City, in painful exile, anxious for her return. They wrote to each other constantly, and talked on the phone.

Finally, almost shockingly, he had found something that meant as much to him as his career. His asexual phase was officially kaput. "She was good for Rush," said Louise Adams. "She made him happy. She was very attractive and nice, and I think he was very proud to be with her. She was very mature." Still, according to Adams, Rush was worried about the age gap.

But it didn't prove to be a problem, at least not in the early years. In fact, Michelle viewed it as an asset to date a more established man. "It seemed attractive, a different world," Michelle said. "It was exciting because I was used to dating college-age guys who didn't have much money. If they took me out, it was for pizza, and a lot of times, I paid. They didn't have a car."

At times, though, the age differential did make her uneasy. "I felt a little uncomfortable when we socialized with his friends," she said. "I felt a little left out, not because they were leaving me out, but because I was still in college and I wasn't going through what they were going through. I didn't have the savvy they did regarding the business world."

Once cemented, the relationship took off in a hurry; much of that was due to Michelle's initiative. It was she who suggested to Rush she move in with him after her return from France in July. She arrived home from the airport, opened her suitcase to unpack gifts for her family, quickly closed it back up, and went off to Rush's apartment. That was pretty bold stuff for a twenty-one-year-old girl from the Midwest. Then, in August, it was Michelle who proposed to Rush. Who cared about tradition? They had been talking in general terms about the concept of a future together when Michelle, never hesitant, blurted out: *"Why don't we just get married?"*

Her parents were not in a position to offer any objections to their daughter's seemingly hasty move. Her mother, a British war bride, had been fifteen when she got married to her husband, who was fifteen years *older*. So they couldn't exactly bring up the age issue, either. "I guess they felt that if they tried," Michelle said, "they wouldn't be able to talk me out of it."

But even if he could afford to buy her more than pizza, Rush didn't have the financial stability to promise Michelle the most comfortable life. He was making little with the Royals, and she was still in college. They knew it was going to be a struggle for the foreseeable future. "In fact," Michelle recalled, "I'm sure we were in debt."

Their first financial sacrifice was the wedding. Instead of holding it in a luxurious hotel or a romantic outdoor location, Rush and Michelle got married on December 19, 1982, in a banquet room at Royals Stadium because Rush, as an employee, could get a good deal. Just under a hundred people braved the Kansas City cold to attend the affair, which didn't take up much time. "It was like eight minutes long," recalled Michelle. "I'm not a person hung up on ceremony." The newlyweds went to New Orleans for their honeymoon.

The Limbaughs and Sixtas came from the same state, but a different universe. The Limbaughs believed in apple pie, the flag, and Ronald Reagan. The Sixtas believed in the Peace Corps and the unions and John Kennedy. In fact, Michelle's father, Rudy, was a proud member of the United Auto Workers.

The philosophical discrepancy never bothered Rush; he has always counted many friends on the other side. But his father, Rush, Jr., the family's top diehard, had trouble accepting liberals into the fold, whether they were in-laws or not, which the Sixtas discovered on one nervous visit to Cape Girardeau.

"I don't know who brought up politics," Michelle said, "but Rush's father went off on my parents. 'How could you be Democrats?' he said. I don't know who calmed them down, but my parents kind of shut up. It was a bit intimidating." Michelle once told *Sacramento Magazine* that because of her liberal background, her parents "want to know what the hell has happened to me."

Ironically, just when he seemed finally fulfilled in his personal life, his mood at work started to go downhill. "The last two years I was with the Royals, I was just flat-out miserable," he told Bob Costas. "I was making less money than I had ever made in my life. It was the only time in my life I had ever judged myself by how little money I was making."

He had expected that hanging out with the ballplayers would be akin to mingling with the gods at Mt. Olympus. "When he first went to work there," said Tom Sullivan, who became a close friend in Sacramento, "he thought the professional athletes were superhumans, and once he found out what they were really like, he didn't think they were all that impressive, and that they were no different from any other group of guys."

Somehow he had also imagined that his presence in the clubhouse offered proof that he belonged among them, but he did not belong among them. He was a low-level employee in marketing and promotion. Likable, to be sure. Need a fun person to have around? Why, call Rush. Want to talk sports? Bring in Rush. Got a music trivia question? That's right, Rush.

But the ballplayers were making hundreds of thousands, and owned the town. Rush made $20,000 and was lucky to own a car. "He was around all these millionaire players," Valle said, "and a lot of them were friends of his and they accepted him as an equal, but yet, he was not an equal and that was kind of sad and he started feeling depressed about it."

Rush did enjoy a few good friendships among the players, including the most revered Royal of all—George Brett. Brett was the first great player in franchise history, a future Hall of Famer. As single guys, they went out to dinner together and talked sports until there was nothing left to talk about. "I always thought he knew as much about sports as anybody," said Brett.

Rush would often come down after games to chat with Brett and a few other players, including Quirk and John Wathan. Brett said the players never looked down on Rush, and would grant almost any favor he asked, although Wathan said that wasn't always the case. "Not everybody at that time was that nice to him," said Wathan. "His job was to ask for autographs and sometimes, there are players who don't like to be bugged to sign autographs."

Rush never had a problem with Brett. In fact, according to Michelle, the Royals superstar once gave Rush some money to help her finish college. She had got way behind financially with her trip to France. (Last year, when Brett had his first child, he joked that the baby looked a little like Rush.)

"He just seemed like a happy-go-lucky guy," Brett said. Rush's philosophy, according to Brett, seemed to be, "'I'm going to do my job, and make my $20,000 a year, and live in my cheap little house in Overland Park, and go on with life.' . . . I never resented him because he was making $20,000 a year. Rush was doing his job, and he was friendly, and he was a nice, sincere guy."

Brett also valued Rush's expertise in electronics. Whenever Brett needed something hooked up in his house, he called Rush. Once, when Rush connected Brett's new answering machine, he couldn't resist adding an extra component. "He'd do his Howard Cosell imitation on the recorder," Brett said, "and it sounded just like him, it was unbelievable. People would call up the first time, and they'd say, 'How'd you get Howard to do that for you? Think he'd do one for me?'"

But Rush was not completely Rush with the players, perhaps because he knew that he wouldn't be totally accepted if he revealed the whole package.

"He had to come to our level," said Quirk, "because we certainly couldn't go to his level." For one thing, he avoided politics, which was no surprise. "There isn't a lot of politics talk in the locker room," Brett joked. "I don't think anyone in the basement [where the ballplayers were] knew how intelligent he was, because he didn't show it." He and a few other players also played football with Rush on Saturday or Sunday mornings in the winter. "He was a lineman," said Brett, "one of those weekend warriors."

To this day, Rush has maintained his close ties with Brett, Quirk, and Wathan, which is one thing about Rush Limbaugh. No matter how successful he's become, he has stayed loyal to his friends.

But, despite his fondness for some of the players, the job was becoming too easy for Rush. "He was way overqualified for that job," said Wathan, "and he felt locked in. He talked about the frustrations all the time, and that he couldn't be creative."

Here was a guy who was a brilliant communicator and salesman, and he was relegated to handling first-ball festivities and corporate get-togethers for people who didn't have a fraction of his intelligence. "He got so bored with it," Millie Limbaugh remembered. "He said, 'What I do, any high school kid could do. There's no talent to this job.'"

Quirk said it was his impression that Rush joined the Royals with the eventual hope of landing a job as the team's play-by-play announcer, but it soon became clear that he wouldn't dethrone the incumbent duo. "Once he got in, he realized that Denny Mathews and Fred White were institutions there," Quirk said.

Adams said Rush was also interested in possibly doing some announcing on the public address system, but even that didn't come together. "We had a PA announcer who never missed a game," Adams said. Confined to his corporate duties, Rush wasn't directly involved with the fun part of working in baseball—trying to win ball games. Sometimes the decision makers in the baseball end of the organization felt strange talking about the intricacies of the game to someone in promotions. He was so unhappy that part of him was relieved when the Royals failed to make it into postseason play. "He wasn't it, he wasn't the deal," said Kit Carson, his current chief of staff, "and Rush always wanted to be the deal."

Yet, despite his frustrations, he stuck with the Royals, perhaps hoping for a promotion someday. That chance came when Burns, his friend and boss, landed a job with Baseball Commissioner Bowie

Kuhn in the summer of 1983. "It was tough for him when I left," Burns said. "We were soul brothers." The two talked shop, and listened to jazz together. When Burns left, Rush felt abandoned.

Still, as his assistant, Rush assumed, and quite justifiably, that he would be a logical choice to move up in the organization. It would mean a pay raise, a more prestigious role, and an opportunity for the respect that he still sought from home. He and Burns held long discussions about where they wanted to be in life, and Rush was certainly not even close to his destination. This promotion could bring him closer.

But the position went to Dennis Cryder, an outsider from the National Collegiate Athletic Association. The Royals felt Rush was not upper management material, and certainly lacked the experience to tackle such a broad and complex assignment. "He wasn't cut out for it," said Dean Vogelaar, who worked in public relations. "You could see from our standpoint that it wasn't going to happen." For Rush, the rejection was the final, ultimate humiliation. "He had to tell Michelle that he didn't get the job," Louise Adams recalled, "that they hired someone from out of the building." Replied Michelle: "That's when he developed an attitude problem."

Rush claims, however, that he never really wanted the job in the first place. "I was going nowhere," he told Costas. "I was so angry and so disgusted, primarily at myself, that I didn't want it, and I made a half-baked attempt at getting it and failed."

Rush also came to the sobering realization that he had no future in baseball, and if something didn't happen soon, he could be stuck forever in a low-paying, dead-end existence. Everyone in the organization was sympathetic. They knew his true calling. "Those who were closest to him," recalled Adams, "told him he was wasting his talent here. He wasn't using his voice."

He was at the lowest point of his life. "After five years of PR work, I was earning $20,000 a year," he told *Success* in 1993. "I'd already failed at the one thing I really love, radio. Now I'd failed at the 'real job' which was supposed to make me a 'real person.' I was looking into the future and I saw absolutely nothing. I had no idea what I was going to do, who I was going to call . . . I was 32 years old, making less money than I earned at 21. I was empty, directionless and futureless."

Then, if possible, he slipped even lower. He was out of work. "I knew the old way of doing things," Rush told Costas. "Dennis [Cryder] as a new marketing guy with the desire to put his own stamp, thought it would be wise to be alone or get someone new who was part of his new regime, so I was asked to leave. I was given two weeks. Herk Robinson [general manager] took me over to the Sheraton Royal Hotel, and we had lunch. Nobody wanted this to happen. It wasn't that they disliked me."

Michelle was devastated by the news. Rush's ego might have been deflated, but she was more concerned with their bank account. "I didn't know how we were going to pay our bills," Michelle said. "He told me, 'Michelle, if you ever start getting an attitude in a job, leave before they fire you. It's better that way.' "

Now what? Radio didn't work, and his move into the corporate world didn't pay off, either. "He had a tough time trying to figure out what he was going to do," Michelle said. Rush, in an interview with Costas, admitted: "I was despondent at radio. I thought I had failed. I was seriously thinking of going to work for Guy's Foods, a potato chip company in Liberty, Missouri. I was going to sell potato chips, not drive the route truck. I was going to be a management guy for $35,000 a year. I was looking at that as Nirvana . . . I came so close to abandoning what made me the happiest."

Thankfully, for Rush, that particular Nirvana never came. Taking the advice of a good friend, who told him to follow his only true passion, Rush cashed in on his contacts in the radio business; it was his last chance to be happy. "Fear and need are tremendous motivators," he told *Success*. "I couldn't go on living like this. So I decided to go back to what I loved." His family, however, according to Michelle, was praying that he would make a different choice. "That was a terrible scene," said Michelle.

His five years with the Royals, however, was not a wasted experience. Rush saw what life was like on the other side of the microphone, giving him a new perspective that has served him well since he returned to radio. "I met people I would never otherwise have had the chance to meet," Rush said in a 1991 interview with the *Squire*, a Kansas City weekly publication. "How many people get to go on the field or sit in the dugout or go to the clubhouse or be in the press box? They are memories to me. I learned business—I never knew business."

Yet, leaving the Royals was the best thing that ever happened to him. Otherwise, he might still be in baseball, which would probably make him far from the most dangerous man in America.

7

ONE OF HIS CONTACTS WAS RAY DUNAWAY, THE morning disc jockey at KMBZ in Kansas City. Because of his responsibilities with the Royals, Rush met regularly with jocks to help promote the team. KMBZ was an especially important connection because it broadcast the Royals games, and good PR meant good ticket sales. Every few months, Rush and Dunaway met for lunch. The conversation would be fairly routine until something happened to uncork the excitement that the radio junkie, masquerading as a salesman, still felt for the profession he had left behind.

"I can remember one rainy spring afternoon, in 1980 or 1981, when a Dire Straits song came on," Dunaway said, "and there was a feeling from Rush that he thought he could do better than the jocks on then."

In the fall of 1983, Rush told Dunaway he wanted to come back to radio. Dunaway had been a big fan ever since he heard Rush one night in the late 1970s on KFIX. "He was talking to a woman about the ERA amendment," Dunaway recalled. The woman was arguing that the deadline for getting enough states to ratify it should be extended when Limbaugh "used a football analogy, saying, 'You're behind in the fourth quarter. What are you going to do? Ask the referee for another quarter?' I thought that was rather unique." Rush and Dunaway became good friends. Dunaway, after all, with a big salary and a high profile, was who Rush wanted to become.

With Dunaway's urging, Rush called program director Phil Mueller. "I talked my way in there," Rush told Costas. Soon, after nearly a month without work, he was back on the air. Michelle could rest easy. The bills would get paid. The ego would get massaged. The husband would be fulfilled. "He was like a lot of guys who have been in the business for a long time and never made a big mark," said one KMBZ colleague. "He was frustrated and trying to find a way to make a good living."

His first assignment was to read the news. "We were pretty excited about hiring him," said Russ Wood, who was general manager of KMBZ. "He was obviously capable of handling the radio situation."

Finally, Rush Limbaugh would be Rush Limbaugh, not Jeff Christie. He would become the respected journalist telling everyone about Reagan and Gorbachev, not the overlooked disc jockey flipping meaningless records from the past. He would now become an important component of a radio station hoping to pride itself on in-depth reporting and commentary. He might even become the serious conservative thinker he and many others always perceived him to be underneath all that bluster. Whatever might happen at KMBZ, Rush was elated to be back at the only place he ever belonged. He knew that he would be haunted forever until he returned to radio. He still had a hell of a lot to prove.

He was a new Rush Limbaugh, mercifully liberated from the burnout and disillusionment of the late 1970s. He was no longer naive about the business of radio, fully aware that no job would ever be safe. But after seeing the world from the other side, he figured he might as well stick with what motivated him, eternally unpredictable as it might be. "I came to the point where I decided, 'Just do the best you can, Rush,' " he stated in an interview with his hometown newspaper. "I know it sounds like Miss America or something, but it was at that point in my life that I began to enjoy success."

In the beginning, he was a straight news anchor. Just the facts, Rush. KMBZ had recently switched to a news-information format, and to be taken seriously, it was important to adhere as closely as possible to the program. But asking Rush to confine himself to the nuts and bolts of a news story would be like asking Sam Donaldson to be subtle; it simply ain't gonna happen. Almost immediately, Rush injected his conservative views into each day's broadcast and looked like he might get in deep quicksand again.

"It wasn't all bad," Wood remembered, "but it was causing us a little heartburn because here we had designed this format," and didn't want to change it to fit Limbaugh's style. "We were trying to run more of a straight news/weather/sports/traffic clock, and he was inserting more than what we wanted."

Yet Wood and Mueller recognized the sheer talent and enthusiasm in their new employee, and didn't want to risk losing him to a competing station. Furthermore, they were shrewd enough to anticipate that a strict news format, without any entertainment, was going to fare poorly in the ratings. So realizing his greatest value, they gave him an opportunity to deliver two-minute daily commentaries about local and national events.

"We decided that maybe we ought to create a forum for him to be able to do these type of things," Wood added. "We gave him more freedom so he didn't have to be hampered by a standard news clock." According to Dunaway, the commentaries "had incredible impact, both positive and negative." He cited the time Rush compared the Rev. Jesse Jackson's campaign for the presidency to singer Michael Jackson's 1984 Victory Tour. The point was that both Jacksons are merely entertainers. The point was hilarious, and got a lot of laughs. Even the commentaries, however, were not enough to pacify Rush. He needed a bigger stage, and the station gave it to him. In May 1984, he was made host of the afternoon show, replacing Curt Merz.

Finally, Rush was in his element. He could pick the guests—Rush has always been known for favoring those at his end of the political spectrum—and navigate the tone and thrust of the show in whatever direction he wished. Like his father, who controlled the living room, preaching to those who wanted to be enlightened by The Truth, Rush controlled the airwaves for a few hours each weekday.

No target was immune to his acerbic wit. "I can remember that Louis Farrakhan [the Black Muslim leader] was mentioned at every commentary," said Mary McKenna, who was the news anchor during Rush's show. One especially memorable Limbaugh sermon harped on the city's popular downtown shopping area, the Country Club Plaza, which had begun to feature more upscale shops like Saks Fifth Avenue and Gucci. "It's where people with dough, or people who want to pretend like they have dough, shop," said KMBZ's John Wozniak.

Rush did a piece saying that ugly people should not be allowed on the plaza because it would destroy its reputation as a haven for the beautiful people. He was joking, of course, but not everyone, especially the proud storeowners, took it that way. "Part of the problem," Dunaway said, "was that what he did was satire, but at that point, he still hadn't developed the mechanics for letting people know it was satire."

Another controversial subject was the local football team, the Kansas City Chiefs. One day Rush complained that the team didn't care about its fans because of its policies toward television rights and ticket prices. Whether he was accurate or not, the timing couldn't have been worse, as KMBZ was negotiating with the Chiefs to carry their games for the upcoming season.

The Chiefs' president called Russ Wood, and the conversation wasn't about the team's linebacking corps. "He was upset that our station would say something to that effect, and I assured him that I didn't even know it was being said, that no offense was meant to the Chiefs, and that it was the opinion of Mr. Limbaugh."

Even Rush, though, had some limits. When, off the air, Wozniak joked with Rush that he wouldn't tackle the real critical issues of the day, such as handicapped parking, he knew enough to stay away. Wozniak asked Rush why cripples should be allowed to park closer to the entrance of a shopping mall when it was the able-bodied consumers who spent their hard-earned cash. "He wanted to survive," Wozniak said.

Around the office, he was the same old Rush. Combative. Entertaining. Insecure. Especially insecure. After his shift, Rush spent many hours at the station typing his commentaries for the next day. "He'd be reading them for everyone," Wozniak said, "including the girls who answered the phones. 'What do you think? What do you think?' He was looking for anybody to say 'That's great.' He really needed stroking . . . He tried to compensate for his poor looks by working hard, and trying to be seen as some kind of thinker. I don't think anyone who worked with him ever considered him a thinker."

As usual, Rush stood out as the station nerd who lacked something in the personal appearance department. "The way he dressed," Wozniak said, "if he did come from money, it was money without taste. He wore these slacks, like somebody you'd see at a bowling alley. I didn't get the impression he had a fantastic education or any great depth of knowledge through travel. He seemed like a regular guy who was good with words."

He was also good at schmoozing. Dunaway recalled that, in 1984, when the two covered the Democratic Convention in San Francisco for the station, Rush worked the room like a veteran politican. "He would spend hours at the hotel, where the Missouri delegation was, and he'd eat, drink, and sleep politics. I was struck with how much this guy loves the arena of politics."

Still, his engaging personality couldn't protect him from controversy. Gradually, he was making more enemies than friends in the Kansas City community, especially among women. The National Organization of Women considered him Kansas City's premier sexist media commentator. Rush said that women only care about how much money a man makes, and he joked about what might happen to the country every twenty-eight days if Geraldine Ferraro ever became president. NOW, however, didn't launch much of a campaign against him. "Maybe I just thought he was a harmless nut," said Barbara Crist, ex-president of the NOW Kansas City branch.

Several times a year, representatives from civic organizations met with television and radio stations in order to figure out ways to improve the city. Stations set up these sessions to better assess how to handle the public's most pressing concerns. Plus it was a great PR move. "Time and time again during his brief tenure," said Barry Garron, the television and radio critic for the *Kansas City Star*, "Limbaugh would always be listed at the top or near the top of the biggest problems in Kansas City. They complained about the polarizing attitude, the inflammatory remarks." The *Star* also received numerous letters from outraged citizens who argued Rush discriminated against blacks and women. One listener called the station and threatened to shoot Rush if KMBZ didn't take him off the air.

Garron was no convert to the Limbaugh cause, either. In 1984, in a column, he wrote a mock letter to Rush. Garron was incensed when Rush had suggested that Massachusetts Senator Edward Kennedy would make a great leader for the Soviet Union. ("More people have died at Chappaquiddick than have died in nuclear power accidents," Rush said on the air.) Garron also took offense when Rush told another radio colleague not to mention Eleanor Roosevelt in his presence for fear he would be forced to launch into a tirade against the woman.

"The problem is that you are being paid to offer listeners commentary and your listeners are being sadly shortchanged," Garron wrote to Rush. Nearly a decade later, Garron defended his attack, saying he wrote his column to "put myself on record that this guy wasn't very good for Kansas City and wasn't very good for the station, and having said that, I declined to give him any additional publicity."

Garron added that Limbaugh "expressed such outrageous opinions that you wondered how any kind of responsible management would let this guy on the air, and then when they kept coming day after day, you had to wonder what was going on here . . . that he would suggest that Kennedy would be a good leader for Russia, essentially implying that the man is so liberal that he's a Communist, made no sense." (These days, nearly a decade later,

Rush, as well, despite all his phenomenal national success, still seems disturbed by Garron's attacks. "Barry said I would never make it in Kansas City," he told the *Squire*. "He said the way I did things was in violent opposition to the way people here liked things on the radio. There is a small part of me that says, 'Hey, Barry take this.' ")

But Garron wasn't the only one who had questions about Rush's approach. As the criticism against him began to mount throughout the community, the management at KMBZ was beginning to have its own doubts. First, they tried to tone Rush down, which was like trying to hide Mount Rushmore behind a rock. "I don't remember a lot of toning down," said McKenna. Most of that dirty work fell to Wood, who hardly relished these confrontations with his stubborn employee. "I told Rush, 'Hey, you have to realize we don't live in a vacuum here. We've got to have some consistency of what we say and think of the consequences, and this is simply not an open forum for you to say anything,' " Wood said.

Rush, as always, was offended by the slightest hint from above that he didn't know what he was doing. How could those guys possibly know more about how to put together an entertaining radio show than he did? The challenge for Wood was complicated: How to give Rush the freedom he so desperately required, and yet convince him to conform enough to keep advertisers from screaming for his termination.

The clock was not on Rush's side. Already, companies, including the influential J. C. Nichols Company, which owned the Country Club Plaza, were threatening to pull their spots if he didn't back off, plus there were some major rumblings of discord within the corridors at KMBZ. "There were people inside the building," Dunaway said, "who were not happy with what was going on, particularly his antifeminist positions. Our sales department at the time was largely full of women. Our manager was a woman. He just didn't have a lot of support."

Wood, in one particularly candid talk with Rush, made it apparent that if he continued with his irresponsible attacks, he might even lose his job. From then on, it seemed, Rush's sense of insecurity, already well-entrenched from his youth and the firings in Pittsburgh and Kansas City, made him even more paranoid.

"Whenever anyone was called to the mount, as we liked to say when you were called in to talk to the general manager [Wood], and you came out of the office," McKenna said, "Rush would always make a point of stopping you in the hall because he was sure that his name had been brought up, and you were discussing him." She said he seemed stressed out almost constantly. "He kept the makers of Tums in business."

Dunaway had never met anyone like Rush. "He wanted that job badly," he said. "The feeling that death [losing his radio job] was imminent was rather frightening to him, 'cause he had worked a long time to get back in."

Rush didn't restrict his fears to the office. Almost every night, at nine o'clock, the phone would ring at the Dunaway home, and it was Rush, wanting to go over the day's events and what the most recent forecast might be on his future at the station. "He'd say, 'Think they're going to fire me? What's going on politically?' " Dunaway recalled. He also called the station manager's secretary every night, too, to get her assessment of the situation. He was like a patient diagnosed with a terminal illness searching for the one contrary opinion that would give him some hope. He never found it.

Still, he didn't surrender. He continued to devote all of his time and energy to the afternoon show, arriving hours early each day to read his regular assortment of newspapers and prepare for the controversies that surely awaited him and his listeners. "For me, it was constant support," Michelle recalled. "His ego would go up and down a lot."

The anxious atmosphere at the station also carried over into Rush and Michelle's social life. They could never feel completely comfortable around other station employees. "You really had to watch your back because there was competition," Michelle said. "I was taken aback at one party we were invited to, when one of the other men who worked at the station had a little bit too much to drink, and basically used Rush as the brunt of his jokes, making fun of what he was doing on the air. He was trying to make it seem like they were jokes, but he was really cutting down Rush in front of everybody."

8

RUSH, AS HE SAW IT, FELT HE WAS MERELY DOING what he was asked to do. The station had hired a consultant named Norm Woodruff from San Francisco, who had been responsible for turning the all-news KCBS into a big winner. KMBZ brought him in for an encore performance.

When he arrived, he told Rush to be a rabble-rouser, to generate as much controversy as possible, which, of course, was no trouble for the host; Rush could create controversy in his sleep. The trouble was, however, that, at the same time, people like Wood were getting a lot of pressure from advertisers and civic groups either to dump Rush or control him. "The consultants were telling him to go for it," Wozniak said. "The management was giving him signals to cool it. He was in the middle."

McKenna, like other KMBZ colleagues, believed the problem was that management never clearly defined Rush's role. "They [the station] hired him to be controversial," she remembered, "and I don't know if they knew what that meant when they said it." Wood rejected that opinion, insisting the issue was a matter of degree. "His idea of controversy and mine were not the same."

By the fall of 1984, neither Wood nor Woodruff was still affiliated with KMBZ, and Rush was almost on his own. Management was shuffled around, and that's never a good sign for the on-air talent, who collapse like dominoes when stations want to make wholesale changes. Rush told Michelle that the turn-over was pretty typical in radio.

In September, the station hired Andy Ludlum to be director of news and programming, replacing Mueller. The arrival of Ludlum, it turned out, sig-naled departure for Limbaugh.

"For some reason, Andy and Rush didn't get along," Dunaway said. "Andy put him through the wringer, and became very sensitive to Rush trying to put his political views in there. Rush couldn't be Rush and comply with what Andy wanted." Rush told the *Star* that two days after Ludlum took over, he was handed a memo five minutes before his air shift, which in effect said, "you either shape up or you're out."

The memo also, according to Rush, told him to keep political opinions and personal attacks out of his commentary, to refrain from sounding stiff and formal, and to curtail unproductive verbal exchanges with other personalities on the air. Garron said the station wouldn't comment on the memos, but it seemed pretty obvious that "they were looking to build a case to ease him out, particularly in the last month."

The next memo, Rush said, which came a few days later, told him to stop using "therefore" and "so forth" because it cluttered the minds of listen-ers. These hardly constituted the worst infractions ever committed on radio. "Maybe by building a mountain of memos, they could make a case that they had tried to work with him, but it failed," Garron said.

Rush told the newspaper he would try to work harder, and would seek coaching on his own time. Once again, Rush's personal life was the price for his obsession with radio. One KMBZ colleague said that Rush never talked about Michelle. "I don't think they had much of a life together," he said.

On September 18, the most ominous memo yet came from Ludlum. "Unfortunately, I cannot share your enthusiasm for your performance," it said. Anybody with the slightest common sense knew that Limbaugh was about to be canned.

Except, it seems, the victim himself. He was turning denial into an art form, and who could blame him? This firing would be the worst yet. But a few days later he was gone, and there was no denying that. "I really believe that Rush was puzzled why the ax came down," McKenna said. He told Garron that his performance as a host, according to the station, "did not meet the standards for what they desired . . . I was one of the few people over there who had a positive attitude from day one."

But he wasn't getting positive ratings, and that might have been what really cost Rush his job. "If you're controversial and that generates cash, that's one thing," Wozniak said, "but if you're controversial and you generate no cash, that's completely different."

In recent years, Rush has indicated on the air and in print that he was "fired by the Mormons," referring to the fact that KMBZ was owned by Bonneville International, which was run by the Mormon Church. Wood claims the Mormons rarely interfered with station business, and "probably didn't even know he was an employee."

Wozniak remembers it much differently. He said the station usually had a Mormon somewhere in the building to report back to headquarters, which was very concerned with the content and financial success of KMBZ.

Regardless of whoever made the final decision to fire Rush, the Mormons or Ludlum or anybody else, the outcome was devastating for him. After the firings in Pittsburgh and the futility of the job with the Royals, KMBZ had granted him another chance, perhaps his last, to live out his childhood fantasies and become a hometown hero. But now, for reasons he considered petty and outrageous, that chance was being taken away again.

When the news became official, Rush phoned everybody, perhaps hoping their support might change the truth. Ultimately, nothing could change the truth and Rush's fragile emotions could no longer be contained. "I remember him crying in the hallways," Wozniak said. "I think he had the impression that it was the end of his radio days. I saw him hugging a couple of the secretaries in the hallway." Dunaway said Rush called him up in a fit of anger. "He said, 'You prick, you knew I was going to get fired.' "

His friends at the station remained sympathetic to his plight, and to this day, defend his courageous stand against management. But radio was radio, and everybody knew that. They were just hoping they wouldn't be the next domino to fall.

Tom Leathers, publisher of the *Squire*, said it was almost inevitable that Rush would fail at KMBZ. "In those days, he let it all hang out about local people and local sacred cows," Leathers said, "but it just couldn't be done." KMBZ, ironically, broadcasts Rush's national show these days, and if there's any controversy, station executives can say, according to Leathers, " 'Hey, it's not our show. That thing comes out of New York.' But if the show comes out of your own town, you got to bear full responsibility for it, and that was difficult in those days 'cause the talk shows weren't that big, and the controversial talk show was not in that much. The marketplace just wasn't ready for a local talk show that did that sort of thing."

9

WAS THIS THE END FOR RUSH LIMBAUGH III? HE was only thirty-three, yet he had already endured a long list of letdowns, of people he didn't respect controlling his fate. He rebelled against his father by dropping out of college and driving his Pontiac halfway across America in search of a dream, but, in comparison, that was easy. He was only twenty, and the future belonged to him. Now, he was approaching thirty-five, that artificial crossroad between a man's apprenticeship and his achievements. He was running out of time, and he had to deliver. "We were worried," Millie Limbaugh said. "We wondered what in the world was going on."

On a financial level, things didn't look as bleak as when Rush left the Royals. "We were coming out of the woods because I had been working for a little while [she had a job for a screen printer]," Michelle said. "It wasn't as bad because now he knew what he wanted to do. When he was back in radio, he was on a track. He knew he had an interest in the news-talk format. At least he had some direction, so it wasn't as scary for me."

Fortunately, for Rush, he had one guy who still believed in him, who was willing to risk his reputation by promoting him as the next great talk show host in America. Rush's career was saved by Norm Woodruff. Woodruff was not always a popular fellow. In fact, some of the staff at KMBZ felt he could be cruel and vindictive, and celebrated when the station and he parted ways. "He was one of the meanest men I had ever met," said one employee.

Even Limbaugh couldn't avoid confrontations with the brash consultant. One day Woodruff was angry about something Rush did in the studio when he blurted out: "Well, we can just hire some people from Wichita to do this for $25,000 a year." The ever-proud Rush didn't miss a beat. "Bring them on." Woodruff backed off. Advantage Limbaugh: The guys from Wichita never arrived.

Woodruff, who maintained close ties to a lot of people in the business, had become a consultant at KFBK in Sacramento, California. The vacancy came when Morton Downey, Jr., who may have invented controversy, did something outrageous, even by his flimsy standards.

On the air, Downey told a cliché joke about a Chinaman working on the railroad, real bottom-of-the-barrel kind of humor. But City Councilman Tom Chinn, of Chinese descent, wouldn't let the moment pass. He called the station to complain about Downey's ethnic slur, and demanded an apology, which the host, of course, would not offer. Chinn was good friends with station owner C.K. McClatchy, which meant big trouble for Downey.

Paul Aaron, KFBK's general manager, only wanted to suspend him for three days, but McClatchy favored a more severe punishment. "He said, 'Paul, at five o'clock today, there is either going to be one vacancy or two, and you get to decide which,' " Aaron said. "That was the end of Morton."

But that hardly meant it was the beginning of Rush. After all, look at his track record. Who *didn't* fire him? But Woodruff, ever the optimist, decided Rush was the guy to replace Downey, but he needed to clean up his act. Not his radio style; that was almost perfect, requiring only some fine-tuning. No, Woodruff went after Rush's appearance, which was far from perfect. It needed some work.

Since high school, Rush hadn't paid too much attention to his looks, except when he went on one of his periodic diets, and they never lasted very long. He was far too consumed with the newspapers, his technological gadgetry, and the Pittsburgh Steelers to care about how he dressed.

Presto, enter Woodruff into his inner circle, and all that changed. Woodruff made sure Rush wore the right suits and that his shoes matched his socks. No more polyester. "The story I hear is that Woodruff taught him how to dress, what to say, and what not to say," said Wozniak. David Fowler, who was a close associate of Woodruff, said the consultant reinvented Rush to match "how he looked and acted with how he sounded." Woodruff felt that a radio personality conveyed more authority on the air if he showed more class in his appearance.

One more thing about Norm Woodruff. It would probably escape notice if the man he had dressed up and presented to the world weren't Rush Limbaugh.

But it is Rush Limbaugh, the self-proclaimed guardian of family values on America's airwaves, the man who told his audience in Sacramento that homosexuals liked to stimulate themselves sexually with gerbils, and later was accused of trivializing the whole AIDS epidemic. The irony is inescapable: Norm Woodruff, who arguably salvaged Rush's career, died of AIDS in San Francisco in the mid-1980s. He was gay.

Yet, since Rush soared into the national spotlight in 1990, the articles in newspapers and magazines, with or without Rush's authorization, rarely mention Norm Woodruff. Rush gives plenty of credit for his success to his mother and father, to Bruce Marr, the consultant who helped get him hired in Sacramento and was the first to envision Rush as a national figure, and to Ed McLaughlin, the former president of ABC Network Radio, who, of course, brought him to New York and made all that possible. It's almost as if Norm Woodruff never existed.

"I keep waiting," Wozniak said, "for Rush to say, 'You can't call me a homophobe because my career, in essence, was made by a homosexual.' Either I have a misunderstanding of how important Woodruff was to Rush, or there's something Rush doesn't want to talk about. It's kind of a mystery to me."

Another question is: Why would a guy like Woodruff tolerate someone who seemed to represent everything he opposed? Fowler has the answer. "Norm was a very strong believer in the marketplace of free ideas," Fowler said, "and that radio was the place to air those differences of opinion . . . Norm was extraordinarily prudish, almost to Victorian fustiness. He never discussed his religion or orientation to any degree with anyone."

Woodruff understood the radio business and the McClatchys, and had no trouble getting Rush in for an interview at KFBK. Marr, serving as a consultant for the station, was immediately impressed by this new voice from the Midwest. "I thought he was a superstar," Marr said. Aaron was equally turned on by Rush. "I was attracted by what got him fired in Kansas City," Aaron said, referring, among other things, to Limbaugh's hilarious ban on ugly people in Country Club Plaza. "I liked that because it showed flair. In our business, you want people to start talking about you . . . He picked up on a local community situation, and got some publicity out of it, and I thought that was pretty creative."

Aaron, narrowing the choice to three candidates, asked Rush to do a trial show one weekend. It went extremely well, and the job was his. He and Michelle were on their way to California.

10

AFTER DRIVING FOR THREE STRAIGHT DAYS FROM Kansas City, the Limbaughs arrived shortly after Thanksgiving weekend, in the heart of the rainy season and without knowing a soul. The Christmas holiday season was fast approaching, and they'd probably have to spend the time in a strange town without their families. The whole situation was a little depressing.

But, on balance, the timing could not have been better for Rush. After all, when he started in the fall of 1984, the station was still reeling from the negative publicity only Morton Downey, Jr., could have generated.

"If [Rush] had just dropped in on the planet, not following Morton," Aaron said, "there probably would have been more of an upheaval, but Morton had blazed the trail and was even more controversial, and there were always people calling and writing the station demanding Downey's hide . . . So when Rush came, even though he was doing things that, by themselves, may have seemed a little more outrageous; because this was a pretty sleepy place, having followed Downey, people were a lot more receptive of his little spoofs."

105

Rush, of course, was still Rush. He was still going to say whatever came to him; he didn't know how to edit in his head. His pet topics—abortion, Communism, the feminist movement, etc.—were not going to go away.

But if not beaten, he was certainly bruised by his past firings, especially the traumatic experience at KMBZ, when he thought he had finally found a place to stay. He wondered if he could ever feel safe again. When anybody in management at KFBK made the slightest negative comment about his show, or even offered constructive criticism, Rush became very insecure. "He was afraid to say anything that would cause him to be fired," recalled Rich Eytcheson, KFBK's current general manager.

Even today, after all the success he's attained, the KMBZ situation still hurts him. "I find it amazing that for all those years I did radio here," he told the *Squire*, "I never did amount to a hill of beans. I will always have an affinity for this place [Kansas City]. I hope the time comes when I can say it really feels the same way about me."

But the fear of yet another dismissal was not going to win out over his conviction that he was the best judge of what was right for his show. In Rush's mind, "there were certain things about the show that no one was going to change," Eytcheson said, "and if they didn't like it, they were going to have to fire him."

That didn't become necessary, although there were some awfully precarious moments at first. Rush would say something outrageous, almost bordering on an ethnic slur, and some of his

KFBK colleagues were concerned he might be a Downey clone, destined to follow his predecessor on the path to self-destruction.

Bob Nathan, a morning drive host who was working at a rival Sacramento station in Rush's early days and later became one of his best friends, thought the first few months might be the extent of the Limbaugh experiment at KFBK. He feared another local embarrassment "wouldn't speak well of Sacramento radio managers."

But Rush Limbaugh was not Morton Downey, which, incidentally, upset many Downey diehards who mourned their fallen comrade. "Rush was a little more levelheaded than Morton Downey," Nathan said. "Morton Downey was more of a performer who relied on ticking people off . . . Rush just wanted to talk to people." Kitty O'Neal, who served as Rush's producer, said Downey was "childish, juvenile, a real John Bircher. I don't think he was as intelligent, clever, or creative as Rush. It's easy to link the two on the surface in terms of being right wing."

Rush also rejected any comparison. "I've never called anyone a bitch on the air," Rush said in a 1988 interview with *Sacramento Magazine*. "I've never slapped someone and thrown them off the show just for the sake of it. Like Mort will tell you, he'll do anything to get a reaction . . . I think what I do has a little warmth and heart to it. Mort can call people names and then go out and smile about it. I can't do it; I would worry about being so cruel."

Several weeks after he started his show, which aired from 9:00 A.M. to noon, he told the *Bee*: "I

want controversy because of the issues, not because
of rudeness or abruptness with a caller. I don't
want people saying, 'Did you hear how he hung
up on that caller?' I'm a very argumentative person, but I do it with responsibility." Rush had certainly matured since the days he routinely hung
up on people at KUDL's gripe line. A few firings
and the realization that he was unlikely to get too
many more chances might have had something to
do with it.

He also had to deal with the problem of name recognition. "People had a hard time with my name,"
Rush told *Sacramento Magazine*. "It's Rush, not Russ,
and I make sure to tell people. I spell it for them."
But even if the public began to get the name right,
that didn't mean they were ready to buy the act.
Rush, like most talk show hosts, struggled in the
early months to build a loyal audience. That didn't
stop him from using up his daily ration of arrogance.
O'Neal said Rush was insufferable in the early days.
She said he would tell listeners how famous he was,
"and no one had ever heard of the guy. People were
like, 'Who is this case?' He was just pompous with
no reason, and then people finally realized it was
his shtick."

Despite any dramatic rise in the ratings, management was very patient with the outspoken new-
comer. Rush was patient, too. "Rush clearly under-
stands that success is a journey," Aaron said, "not
a destination, and as he got more and more success,
he's never envisioned himself as having arrived."
According to Sullivan, one of the problems was
that Rush was far too serious in the beginning.

He wasn't entirely being himself. "The humor part didn't pick up until probably two or three months into it," he said, "and from there, it started really rolling."

Rush also got a tremendous boost of moral support from station colleagues. Upon his arrival, Nathan practically built a shrine to Rush. "I told him he was the best I ever heard," Nathan said, "and probably one of the best in the country, and that amazed him. He had never considered that. He had been told he was good. He was told he was garbage. But he never changed."

Nathan said that there were some in KFBK's management who advised Rush he'd have to alter his routine, that a talk show without guests would never survive in the Sacramento market.

Rush ignored that warning, just as he had ignored the advice from program directors and station managers in Pittsburgh and Kansas City. He usually paid for his defiance with his job. This time, the difference was that he could get away with it. He was given carte blanche by the top management, which gave him strong enough leverage to bypass the pesky midlevel types who always liked to interfere.

"Those first twelve years, I wasn't the show," Rush told Bob Costas, referring to his early failures in radio. "Records or contests were the shows, not personalities . . . I wanted to be the one to find out whether people listen to the radio." Therefore, no guests would be allowed this time. He also realized that Sacramento wasn't likely to attract the most fascinating people in the world. "Rush maintained, and rightly so," Nathan said, "that if you start bringing guests onto a talk show, you'll just bore your audience." In radio, boredom is suicide for the talk show host.

"The great rule of talk shows is that you have to have guests and you have to interview them," Rush told the *Southeast Missourian* ". . . I don't feel comfortable or trusting in that. If you get a bad guest, you're stuck with him for at least an hour. The worst that can happen in radio is for people to tune out. I don't want to take that chance."

But Christine Craft, who also has a talk show, has another explanation for why Limbaugh doesn't like to invite guests: "He's a control freak." Mary Jane Popp, who hosted an afternoon show at KFBK, believes Rush may have simply evaluated his skills and decided he would be better off going solo: "I'm not sure he's that good an interviewer," Popp said. "Rush wants to listen to Rush too much. That doesn't make for a good interviewer. Rush wants immediately to tell you his opinion." In any case, Rush credits Marr with helping him win this fight against management. His future in Sacramento radio would be entirely up to him.

Sacramento, when Rush arrived, like many big and medium-sized cities, clogged up the airwaves with a string of anonymous clones as talk show hosts. "They all took in the parade of authors that had books to sell in town," Nathan added. "Nobody took a stand on anything. Opinions weren't appreciated by management, so it was all guests. Rush was going to have none of that.

It came to pass very shortly that he was the only local talk show on the radio. All the rest of them were gone."

Rush held the same view about the rest of the field in Sacramento. "All the other hosts," he told the *New York Times*, "were doing the same stuff, interviewing the sewage director or the latest carrot cake recipe expert for your holiday party. In three weeks, there was going to be a Presidential election and nobody was talking about it."

Step-by-step, Rush Limbaugh, left to his own destiny, began to conquer Sacramento. His act, raw in Pittsburgh and rambunctious in Kansas City, was finally coming together in California's capital, just as Woodruff and Fowler had predicted. "We thought he was a better fit with that community," said Fowler.

Rush, after a few weeks on the job, noted the difference between the Midwest and northern California. "In Kansas City, the call-in show was something the station had just started," he told the *Bee*, "and I had to tease the audience and make them mad—violate every rule in the book—just to get them to call. They were listening because they were right there on the phone when I'd play a political version of 'Trivial Pursuit.' But, they wouldn't call in with opinions."

"Here, people are much more self-reliant, and you don't have to tease them to bring them in. They have their own ideas and want to talk about them. I think, too, living in the capital city of the most populous state in the nation has something to do with it. These people are familiar with the workings of government. That makes hosting a talk show a joy."

He really didn't have to do much to bring the people aboard. All he had to do was lash out against the liberal agenda, and the calls would come.

His specialty, as always, was the outrageous. He possessed the uncanny ability to say something so distasteful and absurd that it offended the sensibilities of a large portion of his audience, and yet it was delivered with such perfect comedic timing and razor-sharp wit that many of these same people broke into absolute hysterics. Because when Rush goes off on one of his long tirades, even the most well-intentioned liberal usually finds him amusing, and may even side with this so-called fascist on some issues. The same liberal, ashamed at this momentary transgression, looks around anxiously to make sure no one was watching.

Rush never spared any person or place from his sarcasm. One target in Sacramento was the small agricultural town of Rio Linda. The area was nothing special, but Rush found it a useful victim. He decided that when he had to explain certain fundamental ideas, he would simplify them even further so that people in Rio Linda could understand. "Everybody but the people in Rio Linda thought that was the funniest thing in the world," Aaron said. "He then went out and did an appearance in Rio Linda, and everybody loved him and that was the end of that."

Sometimes, however, his attempt at humor backfired. Among the routines Rush introduced at KFBK was the highly controversial "Gerbil Update," whose premise centered on the idea that homosexuals allegedly used the long tails of small rodents for sexual gratification. During this bit, Rush told listeners they had the option of changing stations "if you don't want to hear about this shocking but true news." Rush said he had checked it out with doctors at local hospitals, and found the rumor was true. "It's absolutely sick," he said. When management faced intense opposition from the gay community and other liberal groups, Rush reluctantly agreed to take the accusation off the air, but, over the years, he continued telling friends and supporters about what he considered this flagrant act of indecency. Homosexuals and others denied it, but denials rarely stopped Rush.

He had a satirical update for every traditional liberal cause of the twentieth century, from the feminist movement to the animal rights crusade, to the advocates of nuclear disarmament. Each segment, accompanied by a popular song, worked as a brilliant parody of the particular leftist cause or personality. In Sacramento and New York, he has done updates on such easy targets as: the homeless, New York's Governor Mario Cuomo, Senator Edward Kennedy (Rush put together a song, "The Philanderer," to the tune of Dion's "The Wanderer"), and, of course, feminists.

In 1985, immediately before the march for global disarmament was about to begin from Los Angeles to Washington, Rush originated The Peace Update. Rush never took the peace movement seriously. "These sons and daughters of rich Democrats," he told the *Bee*, "if not paid by communist organizations, are just scared to death that nuclear war will destroy the world. The march makes them feel better and gives them hope. They actually believe that if everyone did away with weapons, there would be peace."

Rush, however, could never be satisfied with pounding out his conservative agenda in straightforward eloquence; he always searched for the humor in an issue, and more often than not found it and exploited it masterfully. With his Peace Update, he spliced in singer Slim Whitman's tune "Una Paloma Blanca," and, according to Rush's book, added some bomb sound effects "just to tweak any long-haired, maggot-infested, dope-smoking peace pansies who might hear it."

Soon, he found out about an Ohio fundamentalist minister who had called a press conference to announce that he had discovered a satanic message in the theme from the television show, "Mr. Ed." Here was an opening Rush could not resist. He told his audience that he had located a satanic reference in "Una Paloma Blanca" by playing it backwards. He said he felt so guilty that he had played it on the air that he probably would resign by the end of the week.

Naturally, the switchboard was flooded with phone calls from fans who actually believed him. (Some people will simply believe anything on the radio, as Orson Welles found out in the late 1930s

Rush Hudson Limbaugh III

(Photo © Penina-San Francisco)

Rusty Limbaugh in 1968, his junior year at Central High. As Rusty Sharpe he was already broadcasting part-time on KGMO-AM. *(Courtesy Jim Grebing)*

The Limbaugh family in the early 1980s: (left to right)
David; Millie; Rush, Jr.; Rush, Sr.; Michelle; and Rush, III.

(Courtesy Michelle Wennerholm)

Rush and Michelle in Carmel, California
(Courtesy Michelle Wennerholm)

Michelle and Rush in London, 1987. Rush led a group of fans on the "RUSH TO LONDON" tour.

(Courtesy Michelle Wennerholm)

Hanging ten in Maui, 1988.
(Courtesy Michelle Wennerholm)

Michelle and Rush at the 1988 Easter Ball. He was at the height of his popularity in Sacramento, about to make the big move to New York. *(Courtesy Michelle Wennerholm)*

Sitting in the Vice-President's box at the 1992 Republican National Convention with (left to right) Marilyn Quayle, Pat Robertson, and Jerry Falwell. The young man from Cape Girardeau, Missouri, has arrived. *(Photo © Steve Appleford)*

when he broadcast "War of the Worlds," alarming thousands with the news that New Jersey was being invaded by Martians.) "One of the Tower Records stores called," Eytcheson said, "and said, 'What the hell is going on here? All these people are coming in and wanting to buy Slim Whitman records because of something Rush Limbaugh said.' We got calls from attorneys claiming to represent Slim Whitman."

The whole episode, Eytcheson said, was another example of Rush's familiar strategy, which he still employs today, of "being absurd to demonstrate absurdity. The whole point was that people get sucked into this fundamentalist Baptist minister's proclamation. People believe this crap, and that was the point he was trying to make."

Rush's first big confrontation with his liberal enemies—the list is probably longer than Nixon's—came during his first few weeks on the job. He has always been one who didn't waste time making an impression.

Local supporters of the 1984 Democratic ticket of Walter Mondale and Geraldine Ferraro were outraged that Limbaugh seemed to be giving much more attention to their opponents, Ronald Reagan and George Bush. They called KFBK to complain. The station management brushed aside their criticism, but Rush was livid. He went on the air and told the backers of the Democratic ticket that if they had a disagreement with him, they should call him directly and not try to go over his head. "Some of the Mondale/Ferraro supporters who were calling in," Rush told the *Bee*, "were so incoherent that, if I were either candidate, I wouldn't want them speaking on my behalf."

Rush wasn't content with blasting American politicians; he had to go after Mikhail Gorbachev, too. While much of the country and the media showered this unexpectedly accessible Soviet president with affection rarely seen for a foreign leader, Rush felt it was a major sham to honor a lifelong Communist, reformist or not. He did regular Gorbachev Updates, complete with the music from *The Empire Strikes Back*, and came up with a term for the American public's love affair for the Russian politician— "Gorbasm."

On one show, according to *Sacramento Magazine*, he read a brief wire story about a new policy allowing Russian citizens to purchase their own homes. "How visionary," he said with more than a dose of sarcasm. "They are actually going to allow them [Russians] to buy their own homes. Isn't that big of Gorbachev?" By attacking Gorbachev, and hence, Communism, Rush was carrying out the Limbaugh legacy of Red bashing. From his living room in Cape Girardeau, Rush had learned from his father that the "Russkies" weren't to be trusted, that Communism was an evil force bent on conquering the world.

Soon, groups were taking numbers to criticize the new right-winger in town. The lineup included the NAACP, the Jewish community, homosexuals, and, of course, the constituency with the longest-running feud against this chubby chauvinist from the Stone Age—women. Each group checked in with its complaints, on and off the air, which, to

Rush, was exactly the proof he sought that he was doing a good job.

"Look, when this place [KFBK] hired me, they knew they wanted controversy," he told *Sacramento Magazine*. "When the negative phone calls started to come in, they [management] looked at it and said, 'All right, it's working.'" Eytcheson said the liberals took the show far too seriously. "A lot of people took issue with his style as much as anything else," he said, "and it took a while for people to catch on with what the show was really all about . . . He seemed to offend virtually every group you could think of."

Some of them were so outraged that they wanted him off the air. Jews, Eytcheson said, initially considered him insensitive to the specter of anti-Semitism, and the NAACP opposed Rush because of his disrespectful attitude toward the Rev. Jesse Jackson—over the years, Limbaugh has even pronounced his name in a disparaging style. "They [the NAACP] believe he is always bashing blacks," Eytcheson said "because of his disdain for a few leaders. He's not a big fan of Jesse Jackson and the NAACP has seen that as an attack on the whole black community, and that is not the case."

Radio station managers are not generally recognized for their composure under pressure. Often when advertisers, politicians, or powerful special interest groups rise in opposition to a program or personality, the stations surrender without a fight. In Rush's case, when the usual suspects—i.e., liberals—began calling for his termination, no rule dictated that Paul Aaron had to defend his besieged employee. In fact, conventional wisdom indicated that the most prudent thing might have been to cut his losses right away before facing the embarrassing sequel to Morton Downey; at any moment, Rush was capable of saying something that could generate the same uproar.

In the past, that's how management dealt with Rush Limbaugh, but not this time. "Paul Aaron," according to Marr, "was a strong manager and he just took the flak and let it ride off his back." Nathan, a veteran of the business, had never seen such feedback for any radio personality. "For most managers, just about all, that would be it," Nathan said. "They'd take him off and bury that controversy. But we had a guy who knew, 'Okay, we have negative. But we have positive, look at the numbers grow.' He wasn't bothered at all by that; he got a kick out of it. He's the guy who brought Morton Downey in."

Meanwhile, away from the turbulence at KFBK, there was life with Michelle, which was significantly more calm. At first, she was a little apprehensive about the move out West; Missouri had been her whole life. But slowly the couple adjusted well to their new surroundings, and began to accumulate friends. KFBK's Tom Sullivan, knowing that Rush and Michelle were new to the area, invited them to his annual New Year's Eve party. They accepted, and quickly became friends with his family. Even after his move to the Big Apple in 1988, and the almost impossible demands on his time, Rush has managed to attend most of the Sullivan parties.

For the Limbaughs, Sacramento was the perfect location, two hours from the mountains, the ocean, the casinos (Reno–Lake Tahoe), and the wine country. Michelle recalled one weekend in which she and Rush, along with Bob Nathan and his wife, were guests at a very classy vineyard. Their refrigerator was well-stocked with food and champagne. The kid from Cape Girardeau, who could have been a rich lawyer but had struggled to pay the bills in Pittsburgh and had made only $20,000 with the Royals, was living like a king. "Rush enjoyed that so much," Nathan recalled, "that he decided that's how he wanted to live. That was my first indication that that was the kind of life that he wanted for himself. He wanted to be somebody."

11

IN SACRAMENTO, RUSH LIMBAUGH WAS SOMEBODY, and the station made sure everyone knew it. As Rush's popularity increased—the ratings made their most impressive leap between 1986 and 1987, to a 13.3 share, far outdistancing any competition—KFBK took full advantage of their suddenly sizzling star. In 1988, he reached a 14.4 share. His closest rival was a soft music station. Translation: He had no rival.

They put him on billboards, teasing Sacramento citizens with the following: "Don't you just want to punch Rush Limbaugh?" (The vote would have been real close.) They asked him to promote everything on the air—it almost became the Rush Limbaugh Network. "Sacramento was the first place in his whole career," Marr said, "where we let Rush Limbaugh be Rush Limbaugh. That's where he really honed his skills at doing what he's now doing."

Success, however, didn't erase his insecurities. O'Neal, his producer, said Rush would always be seeking approval from her. "He always wanted to make sure someone was laughing at his joke," O'Neal recalled. "I always had to pay attention, keep a rapport going. 'Did I think this was funny? Was I interested? Was he getting a rise out of me?' And if it wasn't me, it was somebody else."

Mary Jane Popp was stunned by Rush's lack of confidence. She assumed that anyone who had worked for as many years in the business as he had would have overcome those doubts by now. "It was fascinating that he would ask my opinion, whether I thought the show was good or not," Popp said. "I mean, 'Who cares about what Mary Jane says?' And I used to tell him that, 'Don't care what Mary Jane Popp says! You know what you're doing on the air.' "

He certainly did. Finally, as the ratings kept going up, Rush started to exude more confidence. "He became less paranoid," Eytcheson said. "He's still a very insecure person and not quite sure that people really like him, but he did become much more comfortable at that point, even more coachable than he had been before, and no longer felt that if he said the wrong thing, he was going to get fired."

Throughout his radio career, from Pittsburgh to Sacramento, there has been a wrong way and a right way to coach Rush Limbaugh. His parents had told him to be humble before his superiors, to do whatever they demanded of him. But his parents were never in radio, and lived in a different era.

The wrong way, as his firings demonstrated, was when some all-knowing program director told him in blunt, almost threatening, terms to tone things down. The right way, as Eytcheson employed numerous times, was gently to explain to him that there might be a better approach to get his point across to the audience. Usually, Rush listened carefully to the advice and acted appropriately to improve his show. "I never ordered Rush to stop anything," Eytcheson said. "I found the best way to manage Rush was to appeal to his own intelligence, and not say, 'I'm the boss. You're the subordinate.' "

With his renewed confidence, Rush began to expect preferential treatment from KFBK, and when he didn't get it, he let management know. Once, soon after the station hired the new morning combo of Dave Williams and Bob Nathan, a direct mail campaign was initiated to publicize the station's on-air personalities. KFBK put Williams and Nathan at the forefront of that promotional effort, which made Rush furious. "He felt that he was the personality and the star of KFBK," Aaron recalled, "and that he should have been featured in a more predominant way."

In 1986, when his contract was due for renewal, this time KFBK made certain Rush felt appreciated. Eytcheson asked what it would take to make him happier than he had ever been. He said Rush told him: "You know I've never really felt like I was part of any community. Every radio job I've ever had, I've gotten fired from, and I've never made enough money to own a home. I want to belong. I've never felt like I belonged anywhere." So Eytcheson gave him a bonus substantial enough to make a down payment on a new house. Mission accomplished. Rush was a happy camper.

"When I signed my new contract," Rush told *Sacramento Magazine*, "I got 90 percent of what I wanted. I've pretty much got the freedom to do what I want to do."

According to the magazine, Rush's new pact was for three years, but it constituted only sixty to seventy percent of his annual income, which was close to $100,000. Because Rush Limbaugh, master of conservative rhetoric and preeminent entertainer, was gradually assuming another identity: Rush Limbaugh, salesman.

His experience with the Royals was paying off; he could schmooze with the corporate types as well as anyone, and could sell mattresses and appliances to his audience as well as he sold school prayer and capital punishment—maybe even better. He became a spokesman for a cellular phone outfit, a local jewelry chain, and a bed company. Who needed Willard Scott?

Rush's first client in Sacramento was most appropriate: Nutri-System. Rush, once again, needed to lose a lot of weight, and he loved challenges. As the diet worked, Rush went on television to prove it. "Hi, I'm world-famous radio talk show host, Rush Limbaugh," he said, holding his pants out by the waist to show the difference. But, as soon as he had lost sixty pounds in sixty-five days, and his waist had trimmed to thirty-seven inches, Rush went back the other way. Within six months, he had made up the entire amount. Yet he still talked like a winner. "I got paid because the deal I had was to lose the weight," he told *Sacramento Magazine.* "I never made a deal saying that I had to keep it off."

Soon, Rush had something else he wanted to shed—his growing image as Sacramento's chief huckster. From the beginning, when he first endorsed products on KFBK, that was something Rush was concerned about. But the money and personal exposure, plus the benefits to the radio station, were too valuable to ignore. For a guy who had struggled for years to make a living, the extra cash was a nice reward for his patience, and a huge ego boost.

But there was his reputation as a serious commentator on the conservative scene that he wanted to keep intact, and promoting video cameras and bedspreads could easily put that in jeopardy. "I'm not in the the forefront of a carnival here," he told the *Bee* in 1986. ". . . I was happy to do it at first because I was out to prove my talent. I charged a minimum fee to limit it. But with my success, we get requests from paying clients to have me also read their live commercials. Listeners can't tell the difference between my personal testimony and my reading the copy. I feel my credibility waning every day . . . The other day, a salesman asks me if I need concrete or a Persian rug? What do I need with a cement mixer, and can you picture me helping Iran? I'm not the prostitute; the salespeople are. I don't want to lose the station money, but this has to stop somewhere."

Eytcheson said Rush would carefully scrutinize each company he was thinking about promoting to make sure he believed in its product and principles. Rush was well compensated for each deal, making as much as ten percent of the station's profits on those campaigns. Because of Rush's ratings, advertising rates during his time slot jumped from $40 to well over $100 per minute. He was making KFBK very rich, indeed.

At home, on the surface, he and Michelle were very happy. In 1986, they moved into a new sixteen-hundred-square-foot two-story home with a yard. It was a long way from Overland Park, Kansas, and the depressing life of a small house. For the first time since Cape Girardeau, Rush had become a full-fledged member of the community. He owned a home, enjoyed a high-profile job, and was a spokes-man for some of the biggest corporations in town. He was a pillar. "It was the happiest I'd ever been," he told *Vanity Fair* in 1992. "Sacramento was where I had the gang, where I had a group of friends, where I was as busy and active as I wished I had always been."

Rush and Michelle, to their growing circle of friends, enjoyed an ideal marriage. They laughed together and respected each other. "I thought it was a very equal relationship," said Rich Allen, the deputy director of the California Department of Commerce, who, along with his ex-wife, Meg Catzen, became good friends of the Limbaughs. "He never tried to stop her from expressing her point of view."

One Sacramento observer who got to know the couple said Michelle had a "forcefulness about her. She was not just a sweet young thing. She did not hesitate to interrupt him and disagree with him." On political issues Michelle, not well versed in such matters, usually deferred to Rush, but over the years she began to ask more and more questions and became less and less willing to blindly follow her husband's lead. She was growing up.

But for the most part they steered away from intense philosophical debates. They focused on the common, the routine—going to friends' houses, dining at good restaurants, watching mindless television. (They watched "All My Children" and "Dallas" together.) Believe it or not, Rush even started to sound domestic. "I'm a straight-line, even-keeled guy, who, if you got to know him would probably bore you," he told the *Bee*. "Besides Michelle, my passions are the Pittsburgh Steelers and 'Dallas.' "

Michelle was exactly the model Rush had ordered from the factory. She cleaned his desk at KFBK, and even quit her job in the printing business to serve as his business manager. "It was clear that they were living his life," one writer said. "Everything in their house, from the sound system to his study, was a reflection of him. I didn't see her in the house. It was clear that he dominated her."

This fact hardly escaped Michelle, and as she matured, she began to lose her tolerance for her second-class status. Underneath the facade on display for their friends, the Limbaugh marriage was far from ideal. Rush could talk all he wanted on the air about "feminazis," his characterization of the radical fringe of the feminist movement, and Michelle wasn't going to defend her sisters, but home was a different story. There it was just her and her man, and her man was too busy to pay attention to his woman. Michelle wanted to go to museums and exercise. Rush wanted to play with the new computer universe he installed at home. She did everything possible to help him lose weight, and for a while it worked.

"In fact, we had a membership at a health club in Sacramento," Michelle said, "and I think one of the owners was the one who talked us into going to one of his other clubs—"The Fit or Fat Seminar"— which was a diet that makes so much sense. He was in pretty good shape then. He was trying real hard to exercise." (Later, in New York, Michelle made another effort to keep Rush trim by asking him to walk to work. Rush, true to form, would make it halfway and signal for a cab.)

But Rush didn't stick with any workout regimen. He was too busy with his career. "I think I find it kind of sad in a way that Michelle was left out," said Popp. "That kind of bothered me, because there are ways to incorporate the person you're with. He was so interested in Rush and he was so interested in what was going on that revolved around him, for people to be adoring him. That's okay, because we all have egos, but I think he didn't always look . . . and see how it reflected on other people around him."

There was another problem. Rush had become a local celebrity, which, at first, didn't bother Michelle. "Not having been in the public eye, it was kind of fascinating," she said. But the fascination wore off pretty quickly when her privacy became a casualty of her husband's new fame. "I got accosted once in the produce section of the grocery store because of something that Rush had said," she said, "and luckily, one of my neighbors came up and saved me."

Furthermore, Michelle became slightly suspicious of all the people who wanted to become part of her life. "I just always questioned the friendships that we had and why people were attracted to me," she said. "Was it because I was Rush Limbaugh's wife? Or did they really like me for me? Did they like Rush for himself or because of his celebrity? That was always hard to figure out, but it was always a constant question in the back of your mind."

The power could be intoxicating, and deadly. "I caught myself, and went, 'Wow, I can understand how people in the public eye can get into it, and let their egos get out of proportion," Michelle said. In later years, Rush understood exactly what she meant. "The other day, a guy came up to my mother and practically got down on his knees to thank her for giving birth to me," he told the *Bee*. "Now I know how people like Jim Bakker do what they do."

One day, Michelle couldn't take it any longer. She told Rush about her unhappiness and suggested a cure: divorce.

But Rush, still deeply in love with her and committed to the idea of marriage, if not the spirit of it, talked her out of it. He promised he would change, and told her things would get better, and over time, as their social life expanded even further beyond their wildest expectations, Michelle put that option away. She would give her husband another chance.

12

THAT WAS A LUXURY, HOWEVER, THAT HIS POLITI-
cal opponents weren't as willing to offer. Leading
the procession against his reactionary ramblings on
the air were members of the Sacramento women's
movement. Shireen Miles, the state coordinator of
NOW, was so outraged by Rush's relentless attacks
against feminists—the clinching blow was when
he called the group, according to Miles, a "ter-
rorist organization"—that she asked for an on-air
retraction.

The station refused but did agree to let her and
another female activist break the no-guest rule and
appear on the show live to present the opposing
view. This would make great radio. "We had a
pretty good discussion," Miles remembered. "It
was a legitimate exchange of views." This wasn't
surprising because Rush, for all his posturing when
he's doing a monologue, can be quite civilized
toward the other side.

Afterward, Miles and her friend walked to the
parking lot, satisfied they had confronted the beast
on his home turf and got their points across in a
serious, respectful manner. Then, as they found out

later, the other Rush Limbaugh showed up. He told his audience, "You wouldn't believe what a couple of ugly dogs we were," Miles said.

In one quick strike, Rush had completely shattered the good will established on the air and further crystallized the anger of women who felt he represented the worst in men. There seemed to be little they could do. "You can't call up," Miles said, "because if you do, it just gives him an opportunity to go off on one of his monologues. A lot of people complained to station management about him, and management said that he drew a large listenership, and that pulls in the bucks."

So that was that. Miles said that NOW did try briefly to force Rush's removal from the air by boycotting some of KFBK's most well-known advertisers, but the effort was futile from the start. "We knew the groups he was appealing to wouldn't support the ERA anyway." But undertaking a boycott helped to illuminate the essential dilemma facing many liberals who oppose Rush: Do we have a right to deny him *his* right to speak?

"Most of us are strong believers in the First Amendment," Miles said, "and you realize that, at some level, you have to let him hold his beliefs." Yet, one former KFBK coworker found many fellow liberals intolerant of Rush's brand of militant conservatism: "I'm surprised at the number who don't think he should be allowed to speak, that he should be taken off the air."

That group, undoubtedly, includes many homosexuals. Next to women, gays have traditionally been Rush's most vigorous opponents over the years, branding him a naive and dangerous homophobe for his disparaging comments about their life-style and political activism. Perhaps the most stinging attack they have absorbed from Rush came during his much-criticized "Gerbil Update." To many homosexuals, this completely unfounded accusation was a crude assault on their identity and helped to spread among society the notion that gays were some kind of sexual deviants. Yet, surprisingly, there was no widespread gay rebellion against him. There were no serious talks of boycotts or protests.

"Part of it is that because there are some conservative gay people out there," said Gary Miller, a homosexual, who was county chairman of the Sacramento Democratic Party. "I'm amazed at how many gay people think he's great, who agree with him on other political issues . . . so they kind of overlook his gay issues."

Jerry Sloan could never be accused of overlooking anything Rush Limbaugh had to say. Sloan, a gay clergyman, heard Rush's comments and decided to take his case to the city's Human Rights Commission. "He said something like, 'What we're saying about gerbils must be true. I've not had any irate gay people call to refute it.' So I said, 'Okay, honey, you want to see an irate queen, I'm going to show you one.' " Sloan filed a formal complaint, but soon learned Rush would be taking his act on the road, to New York, so he elected not to pursue it any further.

Miller, however, was disappointed that more

groups did not take active steps to get rid of Rush. "I remember one time I had tried to place a personal ad in the *Sacramento Bee* to find out some of the people who disliked him, and see if we couldn't get together and organize something, but the *Bee* refused to print my advertisement." He was not surprised. The *Bee* was owned by the McClatchy family, who also owned KFBK.

What was good for KFBK was good for the *Sacramento Bee*, and Rush Limbaugh was better than good; Rush Limbaugh was gold. Rush, despite his conservative views, was given plenty of leeway at KFBK, and said he knew exactly why. ". . . The truth is Democrats like money as much as anyone," he told the *Southeast Missourian* in 1987. "The show is making money, so they have been very fair and open-minded with me."

The Gerbil Update was hardly the only example of Rush crossing the line between controversy and tastelessness. In another issue involving the homosexual life-style, Rush repeatedly called AIDS "Rock Hudson's disease," referring to the popular actor whose death first alerted the country to the epidemic. "So they [management] called me in," he told *Sacramento Magazine*, "and said the station was getting a lot of calls, 'so can't you call the disease AIDS once in a while?' So I do."

Nobody has ever questioned his skill at damage control whenever he has gone too far. He has known instinctively when it was time to back off, and shift his calculated rage and irreverence to a different favorite liberal target. Rush was also an expert at taking a potentially embarrassing situation and brilliantly manipulating it to his advantage. He could probably turn Woody Allen into Father of the Year.

The prime example: the case of Rush Limbaugh and the Missing Voter. It all started when Gary Miller went down one day to the County Registrar's Office to check out the party affiliations of candidates running for office in local, nonpartisan contests. Suddenly, Miller had a funny hunch. He decided to look into whether his favorite talk show host, Rush Limbaugh, was registered to vote. The microfilm showed nothing under Limbaugh, but, at first, Miller figured, like many radio personalities, that was probably not his real name, so he phoned KFBK to find out. Miller was shocked. Limbaugh *was* his real name, and as a resident of the county, that's the only place where he would be registered.

Miller leaked the information to the press in an effort to make Rush look like a hypocrite. "I thought it was a riot," Miller said, "because here is somebody who is very political, who tells everybody how important it is to vote the right-wing agenda, and here he hadn't bothered to vote himself . . . all this time, he had been talking about how awful the Rose Bird Court [California's Supreme Court Chief Justice] was, and how we were so glad we got rid of them, and so on."

Mary Jane Popp was equally disappointed in her radio colleague. "All talk shows I've ever done, especially anything having to do with politics," she said, "I'd always say, 'If you don't vote, don't call

me, because you have no right to complain.' . . .
You can sit in your big fat chair watching TV and
drinking a beer and fill out your absentee ballot.
He hadn't voted and he was beating on people
for all these issues. That really bothered me, and
I think it bothered a lot of people . . . he didn't care.
That's the impression I got. There was no interest
there."

So, with the word out, it was now up to Rush
to see how he would manage this minor crisis. No
problem. He managed it so well, in fact, he made
Richard Nixon look like an amateur for the way he
defused the Checkers incident. Rush, according to
one colleague, rented a limousine to take him downtown to vote. He made it into a big spectacle, with
himself, naturally, the primary beneficiary of all the
publicity. "A lesser person would have been a total
apology freak for however long it took to get the
public back again," said a former KFBK associate.
"He turned it around in a major way."

Miller contends, however, that a columnist for the
Sacramento Union told Rush he was going to print
the revelation, but agreed to delay the release of
the story for several days to allow Rush to prepare
a well-rehearsed defense. Miller said Rush tried to
duck out of the situation by claiming he just hadn't
had enough time to go down to the proper office
and register. "In California," Miller said, "it's so
easy to register to vote. All you have to do is
pick up the card from the post office. It doesn't
take any time at all." Christine Craft doesn't buy
that explanation, either. "He valued his country so

often that he didn't bother to register to vote," she said.

Miller also denied that the Democratic Party conducted a major investigation of his past and the voting issue was the only evidence of impropriety it could dig up. "We weren't investigating him," he said. "I just happened to be in the voter registrar's office one day." But Rush was so popular, and so adept at deflecting criticism, that the love affair between him and the people of Sacramento was not damaged by this oversight. Rush was the capital's Teflon man.

Soon it became clear that radio wasn't big enough to contain the opinions of this rare, maverick conservative, who could entertain as easily as inform. The Right hasn't had many people who could do both. Sure, folks like William F. Buckley, Jr. and George Will and Pat Buchanan could articulate their cause brilliantly, but, as comedians, they wouldn't have been able to land an audition with "The Gong Show"; compared to Rush, they were borrring! Rush clearly needed another stage, and along came television to provide it.

Rush was asked to appear three nights a week on Channel 13, the ABC affiliate in Sacramento, to debate the representative from the Left, David Rosenberg, mayor of Davis. Unrehearsed and unscripted, the exchange would take a maximum of three minutes, and feature every hotly contested topic, from abortion and the death penalty to the colorization of films (Rush, the consummate capitalist, was pro-colorization). The ques-

tion wasn't whether Rush could tackle these issues spontaneously—heck, he had proved that
ability in college speech class when he needed
no outlines to demonstrate his off-the-cuff eloquence. The question was whether Rush's charisma
would translate to the tube. The question was
answered fairly quickly: Yes! The station received
calls after each Limbaugh-Rosenberg tussle, and sixty percent of the time listeners sided with Rush's
viewpoint.

"He just blew him away in those debates,"
said Bob Nathan, "because Rosenberg took it
seriously and Rush understood the entertainment
medium." Rosenberg claims that he lost the arguments because the audience was generally conservative, and Rush's followers were more loyal. He also
said Rush was more equipped to debate after three
hours on the radio each weekday. Either way, clearly
the mayor of Davis, like most well-meaning liberals,
was no match for the almighty communicator. "He
didn't have any of the broadcasting savvy Rush
did," said Craft, "so Rush was always perceived
as the winner whether or not he had the better
point."

There were even more worlds than radio and television for Rush, still in his mid-thirties, to conquer.
For instance, print was something Rush wanted to
pursue. For all his unquestionable articulateness,
Rush possessed few credentials as a writer when
a Sacramento senior citizen newspaper asked him
to deliver a bimonthly column. Years later, when
he hit it big in New York, the *Sacramento Union*
offered him a daily front-page column, which Rush

could not resist. The more people he reached, the better.

Another world was public speaking. This field, of course, had been a Limbaugh favorite ever since his grandfather read a book about famous orators, given to him by his sister, and decided to become a lawyer. Rush's grandfather and father were both masters of timing and emphasis. It almost became a battle of who could make the better speech. "People would come up to him [Rush Limbaugh, Jr.]," Millie Limbaugh recalled, "and say, 'Junior, that was a great speech. Someday, you're going to be as good as your dad.'" Well, thousands of somedays had passed, and now, Rush Hudson Limbaugh III was becoming, arguably, as good as both of them.

Everybody wanted a piece of this new voice on the lecture circuit, and he had no trouble reveling in the adulation. "It was another place he could go out and tell people he was famous," Nathan said. Soon Rush was spending almost every weekend somewhere in northern California, speaking to one group or another, reportedly receiving between $300 and $500 for a thirty-minute delivery. Again, nice income if you can get it.

"I didn't even know any of these people existed," he told *Sacramento Magazine* in 1988. "I started to charge as a way of saying no. But now I'm talking to groups like the California Pear Growers' Association and the California Seed and Grain Foundation."

In other words, he no longer had a life outside

his work. Not that he had ever been a Renaissance Man in his previous life; Michelle will testify to that. But, with the radio show, the television debates, and the public speaking duties, Rush Limbaugh—hell, his face was on billboards!—was now as busy and famous as he had dreamed about two decades earlier from his basement in Cape Girardeau.

Finally, he was certain he deserved his father's respect, and would get it. But much to his son's dismay, Rush Limbaugh, Jr., was still not overly impressed with this radio business. Rush would call his father with his latest triumph, and yet would always hang up the phone and immediately sink into the lowest mood, and it was up to Michelle to prop him back up. "Even when he would have good news, somehow, someway, he would come away depressed cause they couldn't look at the positive aspects of it," Michelle said. What irritated his parents the most, according to Michelle, was Rush's continuing inability to be the subservient employee.

"Rush would tell them too much about how he was going about his business with his career," Michelle recalled, "and the things he would say to his boss, and I think they were probably cringing on the other side of the line because, in their day, you didn't talk back to your boss. You do whatever you're told to keep your job, but Rush has always had his own ideas of what he wants to do. That's why he didn't make it through college."

Respect from the person whose judgment and

opinions meant the most to him would have to wait, maybe forever. He was the star of Sacramento, but he was still Rusty, the college dropout who didn't become a lawyer.

13

THE OFFICE AT KFBK WAS ANOTHER PLACE WHERE Rush didn't receive the respect he felt he had earned. His desk was situated near the back entrance to the building, which most employees used because the front door wasn't anywhere near their offices. As such, Rush became a natural punching bag for the people in sales and engineering and news as they started their day. Many of them were card-carrying liberals, and while they may have liked Rush on a personal basis, they were outraged by what he said on the air.

"Almost to the point of violence," Nathan remembered, "you could see their stomachs wrench as they took their shots." Rush, to his credit, fired stinging return volleys, never conforming to popular opinion in the newsroom. One such combatant was David Hall, a reporter who, according to Nathan, "figured his job in life was to get on the air and save the world from Reagan and the Contras."

Frequently, in fact, Rush initiated the action. "He would throw stuff up for discussion," said Hall, "just saying something, and everyone would contribute. 'You can't trust women' was a good one. All of a sudden, he said it, and then everyone descended upon him, and it was a big free-for-all . . . Nicaragua was a big thing. He was for the Contras." Hall said another station employee worked for a religious community that supported Daniel Ortega and the Sandinistas, which really bothered Rush. Rush would also decide when the arguments would end, storming away just in time for him to start his show. He knew how to make an exit.

He also battled with colleagues on the air. Popp, a staunch defender of women's rights, confronted Rush constantly about his unrelenting sexist rhetoric. Unlike other liberals, she was not intimidated by him.

"Once in a while, he'd make a nasty remark about the disabled or the ugly people," Popp said, "and I used to say, 'You ever look in the mirror? You look like a little baby blimp.' " Generally, though, Rush and Popp refrained from name-calling and stuck to the issues. It made for damn good radio. Popp said, however, that Rush was always dwelling on his lack of formal education, and she wonders whether the fact that she was working on her Ph.D. at the time made him want to pick fights with her to prove his superior intelligence.

Rush was so exceptional at defending himself against the merits of any liberal's argument that some opponents, desperate to save face in any way, would start attacking him personally. "When people could not come up with anything substantive to say to him," according to Nathan, "they relied on personal insults having to do with his weight or calling him fascist." (Rush has been compared to Hitler as often as anyone in America. A typical example is the comment from feminist attorney Gloria Allred, who told *Vanity Fair* that she doesn't want to associate Rush with the Nazi, but "I will say that I wish Hitler had been taken more seriously in the beginning. You know what I'm saying?")

Nathan said Rush fielded those kinds of insults at KFBK with "amazing grace," but that the cumulative effect definitely wounded his self-esteem, which, despite his daily ego boosts on the air, still remained relatively fragile. Rush, according to Nathan, seemed most irritated at the fact that such verbal assaults destroyed the credibility of his colleagues. "He didn't feel they were worthy opponents," Nathan said, "and it would hurt him to see other people hurt themselves." He claims there were no worthy opponents for Rush, although that didn't keep people from taking a shot. "It was like being able to walk past a puppy without petting it," he added. "You couldn't walk past Rush on your way into work without saying something."

Flirting was another Rush hobby in his Sacramento days. Some feminists have argued that Rush, ever since he was the portly nonconformist at Central High who couldn't get the girls, especially the more attractive ones, has developed an intense hatred of women, which manifests itself in his constant use of terms like "feminazis." In other words, he is getting revenge for all the girls who rejected him. Rush angrily disputes that notion.

He claims he loves women, and that his litany of attacks against feminists—he says the movement was established to allow unattractive women easier access to the mainstream—refers only to its most radical elements. "There were some women who would flirt with him, and he'd flirt back," O'Neal said. "There was a girl who worked there who would hike her dress up for him, or stick her leg up in the window where he was. I think he doesn't understand women, but I think he loves them."

Nonetheless, whether he loves women or not doesn't matter to the feminists who believe he might truly be the most dangerous man in America. What Limbaugh says each day to millions of people, according to Allred, an outspoken feminist, is "harmful to the condition and aspirations of women . . . If women can be demeaned and trivialized, then women can be attacked more easily. It puts women at more risk, and it makes it more difficult for us to win change because he does have such a large audience. He makes it more difficult for us to win changes in law that we need for women and children."

But the large audience he managed to amass in just a few short years in Sacramento also carried large risks. Rush, like much of the on-air talent in his business, must have known about the film *Talk Radio*, Oliver Stone's tale about a controversial talk show host who is gunned down by a psychotic listener. Death threats were routine, and Rush certainly got his share. He told *Sacramento Magazine* that one guy even followed him all over town. "I finally called the police," he said, "and they tracked down his license plate. It turned out to be a doctor."

On another occasion, O'Neal recalled, Rush made fun of some nut on the air who then called back, promising to come down to the station with a knife and kill him. O'Neal didn't take the threat seriously; she almost regretted it for the rest of her life. The psycho got past the receptionist, and was heading down the hall toward the studio when engineers tackled him, and he was taken away by police.

"Sometimes, there'd be people out in the parking lot waiting for him," O'Neal said, "and he'd go out of his way to avoid them or wait till they were gone, so he wouldn't have to confront them because he did't know what their intent was. Sometimes, we'd have protesters out in front with signs. Usually, they were just characters loitering in the lot waiting for him."

Rush's fears bordered on paranoia. One former associate claims that Rush was so concerned for his safety that he offered to pay someone at the radio station to start his car because he was afraid it was going to get blown up. "He was perceived as being a little hysterical," the colleague said, "and [someone] agreed to start his car for him." No money was exchanged. Another time, at a St. Patrick's Day parade, Rush wore a bulletproof vest to protect himself against would-be assailants. "It was very scary," recalled Michelle, who also wore a vest. Yet even his critics don't blame him for taking extra precautions. These days he is frequently accompanied by bodyguards. "There are a lot of people who would like to blow Rush Limbaugh away," Craft said.

Another barometer of his extraordinary popularity was that radio stations across the country suddenly became interested in taking him away from KFBK. Among the suitors was KMOX in St. Louis, which Rush adored as a teenager, growing up about 100 miles away. That's the station that employed one of Rush's early idols—Harry Caray (a big Rush fan these days)—and would mean a return to the Midwest, at a powerful station that could be heard throughout Missouri.

"I think Rush would have killed for that if they really would've given him a decent opportunity because it was close to home," Eytcheson said, "and he really needed to feel like his parents were proud of him. That would have been the ultimate for Rush." But discussions with KMOX never quite reached the serious stage.

Other offers came but nothing materialized, and that was fine with Rush because, at thirty-seven, he wasn't anxious to move to another city and establish himself all over again. He knew how precarious and frightening that could be. So he stayed put in Sacramento, though he made it clear that he wouldn't be there forever. "Sacramento is a feeder market," he told the *Bee* in 1986. "It is not my final resting place. Everything I'm doing is designed to hold on. Someday, I'd love to be in Washington, D.C. Right now, I want to be happy for once in my life. I'm an infant for talk radio. In a way, I'm just being born."

Bruce Marr held the same aspirations for the infant Rush. Marr, who along with Woodruff was responsible for resurrecting Limbaugh's radio career after the KBMZ fiasco in Kansas City, knew he was a major talent from the start, and was determined to make sure that, in the proper time, the rest of the world would learn his little secret. Marr fielded the offers from other radio stations and represented Rush's interests. (David Limbaugh, being family, has served as Rush's principal legal adviser during his rise to fame.)

From Rush's early days at KFBK, even during the time when management wasn't quite sure what kind of product they had behind the microphone, treasure or tragedy, Marr was busy planning for the day that Rush would graduate to the big leagues. Forget Larry King. Forget Paul Harvey. This new kid, who nobody had heard of, would prove to be better than all of them. He was as bright as they were, and he had a much better sense of humor. Radio, after all, was mostly to entertain.

The first serious offer to export Rush to the rest of the nation came, according to Marr, from people who represented the family that owned Rice-A-Roni in San Francisco. The family apparently owned a ranch in the Sacramento area, and fell in love with Rush. But they weren't broadcasters, and Marr realized they didn't possess the know-how and clout to put a solid deal together. Still, the talk of going national tantalized Limbaugh, reviving his deep-seated ambition. Rush felt the group behind the move was too ideologically driven but maybe next time that wouldn't be the case.

Next time was already in Marr's mind. For months he kept busy working on his real ace card—Ed McLaughlin. Marr knew McLaughlin from their days together at KABC, the ABC affiliate in Los Angeles. McLaughlin had served as head of ABC Radio Network from 1972 to 1986. He was among the best in the business. When

Group Westinghouse purchased KFBK from the McClatchys in 1987, Marr's contract automatically expired, and he was thus free to begin working out any deal he could for Rush. The first person— the *only* person—he went to was Ed McLaughlin, but he was too savvy to play his hand before the precise moment.

McLaughlin had departed ABC to form his own company, EFM Media Management Inc., which was syndicating medical reporter Dr. Dean Edell's radio program. "Every time I would go to New York," Marr said, "I'd stop in to see Ed and would tell him that 'when you get done with clearing Dean in the markets you want, let me know because I know where the next guy is.'"

McLaughlin, naturally, played the game exactly as Marr thought he would. "Who is the person you're talking about?" he asked his old friend. Marr wouldn't tell him. This exchange went on for about a year. "It's none of your business," Marr would say. "When the time comes that we can make an agreement, I'll tell you who it is." McLaughlin was also restricted at the time by a non-compete contract with ABC, which meant he could syndicate only Edell until the agreement expired in June of 1988. Rush, meanwhile, wasn't expecting any instant miracles. "He wanted me to pursue it [going national], but I don't know that he had a whole lot of confidence that it would ever happen," Marr said.

Rush, after all, had a problem truly grasping what he had accomplished in radio. Part of him knew he had the right stuff for the big time; another part was convinced he belonged in the minors forever. The conflict within him was always over which side would capture his soul. Rush was busy presiding over his kingdom in Sacramento when McLaughlin announced he was ready to take a look. "He got Dean Edell to the point where he was maxing out, and it was time to look at someone else." McLaughlin was planning a trip to San Francisco on other matters, and agreed to meet with Marr and Rush for dinner.

The plan for the evening was for the two of them to drive to the city in separate cars, and then Marr would conveniently leave early, allowing Rush, the king of schmoozing, to score personal points with the man who could change his life. That's exactly what happened. After dinner, Rush and McLaughlin went back to the hotel and talked for about three hours. "I wasn't too concerned about his political persuasion," McLaughlin said. "I was more concerned with whether he was genuine. I quickly ascertained that was the case with him."

Rush and McLaughlin had a lovely chat, but lovely chats don't make people with lots of money take huge risks on behalf of unknown talk show hosts from Podunk, and in radio, everywhere but New York and Los Angeles is Podunk. There was one pivotal test remaining: McLaughlin had to hear Rush in action. He had listened briefly to one of his tapes before, but needed to scrutinize him more carefully. He had to know if this guy could play in Omaha.

So he drove to Sacramento and he turned on KFBK; ironically, at one point, McLaughlin had even

considered buying the station. His first reaction to
Limbaugh was not positive. Rush was arrogant.
Rush was pompous. Rush was not what he was
looking for. McLaughlin was ready to go home.
But then he tried to remind himself to think as
an audience member, not a businessman, and the
results were quite different. "There's that direct connection between Rush and the listener," McLaughlin
told the *Los Angeles Times*. "I just knew that if I
asked somebody what they were listening to, they
wouldn't say KFBK. They'd say, 'I'm listening to
Rush Limbaugh.' They might even have difficulty
telling you the station's call letters."

McLaughlin realized that Rush's arrogance on
the air was shtick, not his actual personality. And
it was the kind of shtick that he knew he could
sell to affiliates from Maine to Montana. He also
knew that Rush's ratings in Sacramento were very
impressive for an AM station way up the dial (1530).
He told his lawyers to hammer out a deal as quickly
as possible with Rush. There was no time to waste.
There was a nation waiting to be conquered.

14

BUT IT WOULD NOT BE EASY TO LEAVE SACRAMEN-
to. First, there was his contract with KFBK that still
had another year to go. Second, there was his love
affair with the town that still had, he had once
hoped, a lifetime to go.

According to the contract's terms, the only way
Rush could resign from KFBK before its expiration
in March of 1989 was if he accepted an offer from
a station in one of the nation's top five markets.
Rush was very fortunate that KFBK did not try to
renegotiate his contract or extend the deal before
McLaughlin came around because it could have
changed everything. The opportunity to go national
might never have arrived. Rush has claimed that
he was perplexed and angry at KFBK's seemingly
passive attitude. This is one time, however, that
he has never regretted management myopia.

Rush took advantage of his opening and signed
an option contract with McLaughlin, giving him
the first right to his services from March 1 through
the end of the year. On that day, Rush formal-
ly informed KFBK that he was giving them the
required thirty days notice, but the station let
him stay on the air through June, until all of

the arrangements in New York could be ironed out. They had their reasons. "We pretty much knew we'd wind up carrying his show in syndication," Eytcheson said. "It was in everyone's interests to maintain as much continuity as possible."

Rush was making the biggest gamble of his life, much bolder, in fact, than his decision in 1971 to drop out of college and accept his first professional radio assignment in Pittsburgh. Then he was twenty, an appropriate age for rash actions. This time he was married and had much more to lose. He owned a town, and now he was abandoning it. There was absolutely no guarantee he wouldn't flop at the national level and be stranded again without a microphone. He got a long-term contract, but he knew that he would probably have to make it in one year, or else.

Rush was scared, and distrustful, even of people supposedly on his side, like McLaughlin. "He didn't know Ed McLaughlin," remembered Eytcheson, "and wasn't really certain he wouldn't be taken advantage of at some point. He was nervous about it because Rush needs time to get to know people, to make sure he's really comfortable with them. The fact that his brother continues to handle most of his personal affairs bears witness to the fact that he needs time to really get comfortable with people."

Rush was not happy about leaving Sacramento and his numerous close friends, and, in fact, before McLaughlin had jumped into the picture, there had even been talk about trying to host a nationally syndicated show from KFBK's studios, but Westinghouse was clearly not ready for that kind of ambitious undertaking.

"You really need your show cleared in one of the top ten markets," Eytcheson said, "and it's difficult to do that if you're in Sacramento." At this point, after Rush's amazing success in his first three years, Eytcheson knew it was only a matter of time before he was snatched away by a bigger market willing to shell out bigger bucks. "It was purely economics," he said about why KFBK didn't try to renegotiate Rush's contract.

So Rush could go only one place—the Big Apple, the most logical headquarters for a national talk show. But there was one major roadblock ahead. He needed to receive air time on a local station in one of the top five markets, and still being an unproven commodity—Sacramento was almost irrelevant to most radio executives—he was unlikely to sign with an outlet in a large city until word of mouth—and good ratings—spread.

Therefore, if he couldn't land a local show, he would be held to his KFBK contract and the whole dream of going national would fall through. Eytcheson said KFBK never made any attempt to keep Rush from leaving the nest. "Rush would have been miserable if he had stayed here another two years," he said. "He would have kicked himself in the ass every day saying, 'I wonder what would have happened.'"

Fortunately, WABC in New York came to the rescue. The station had an opening in its 10:00 A.M to noon slot, and McLaughlin, relying on all his years of experience, pitched him brilliantly, fully aware that Rush's career might very well have been riding on his delivery. "They [WABC] had never heard of Rush Limbaugh," McLaughlin said. "It wasn't slam dunk."

But the pitch worked, and Rush agreed to host two talk shows—a local show for WABC from 10:00 A.M to noon, and a national show from noon to 2:00 P.M. WABC supplied the studio, engineers, telephones, and call screeners for both shows. The Rush Limbaugh Phenomenon was ready to roll. "I didn't have specific goals for growth," he told *Success*, explaining why he left Sacramento. "Goals are too limiting. I just knew I wanted more."

Among his closest friends, Rush sounded reborn with his decision to come East. "One Saturday, he called me," remembered Bryan Burns, his ex-roommate in Kansas City, "and said, 'You're not going to believe this, but I think I'm coming to New York." Sullivan recalled a similar euphoria. "He said, 'Tom, don't tell anyone. There's this guy in New York, and he used to be president of ABC Radio' . . . He was so excited." Yet once again there was a definitive gap between the private Rush and the public Rush. For a man on the brink of getting everything he ever wanted, he was remarkably downbeat.

"I decided to leave Sacramento in April, but didn't go till July," he told the *Bee* in an interview shortly after his arrival in New York. "I realized that everything I'd been searching for in 17 years I'd found in Sacramento in the last year and a half. Friends. Security. Stability. A house. I got so depressed, I guess you could say I sat around the house in my underwear, sulking."

His wife, however, wasn't sulking at all. She greatly anticipated the move to New York. After all, her whole life had been spent in Kansas City and Sacramento, and she knew she deserved a more appropriate setting for her widening cultural interests, for a sense of vitality that only a city like New York could provide. She was a graphic arts major who had been to Paris. Sacramento was a suitable detour for a few years, but it was certainly no final destination for someone like Michelle Limbaugh.

Rush, however, was wary of New York. He had been there only once before, with the Royals, and that visit hadn't done much to tame his overwhelmingly negative perception of the place. The small-town boy was worried about the big-town crush. "I think his view of New York was just what you get from watching television," Marr said. "He wasn't sure he was going to like it all."

Burns went around with Rush and Michelle looking for apartments. "He was quite concerned about the various nuances of New York life," Burns said. " 'Oh, my God, New York. Where should I live? How much money do I need to make here? Is the city all it's cracked up to be? Will I do this right? Will I be okay?' " Burns said Rush made the right decision by living in Manhattan instead of the 'burbs. "I bought a house in New Jersey and commuted," Burns said. "I had to have a yard, and I think he was smarter than that."

On a professional level, Rush was equally apprehensive. "It wasn't the money that scared him,"

Nathan said. "He had been broke before, and he was prepared to be broke again. All of a sudden, he's got to survive on his own merit with no help, but he had had plenty of practice by then. I don't think he realized how good he was. He wasn't egotistical enough to think America would respond to him the way they have."

People who knew him well realized that conquering Sacramento had hardly removed all of his inner doubts. "Parts of the false bravado—'The world's greatest talk show host, talent on loan from God'—are really mechanisms to contend with his own insecurity," Eytcheson said. "He's a guy that I think really wants to be liked and appreciated, and still is not quite convinced that he is."

Back in Sacramento, the Limbaughs still had to wrap up the final details of their nearly four-year stay. Rush made plans to start his two shows in New York, while Michelle took care of selling the house, car, and other similar chores. Everything seemed to be going according to plan, as the happy couple was preparing for the big time.

After Rush had already arrived in New York, Carlos and Susie Rodriguez, who had become good friends of the Limbaughs during their last two years in Sacramento, hosted a farewell party for Michelle. "She was with us the night before she left," said Susie Rodriguez. "We went to a Gloria Estefan concert and then we all came over to the house afterwards, and I brought out a silver platter with a big red apple on it, for the Big Apple. We were laughing and joking and everything."

On July 4, the day after the United States shot down an Iranian civilian jetliner in the Persian Gulf, Rush began his local show from WABC. Tom Leathers, a friend from Kansas City, just happened to stop by the studio during Rush's first day, and felt sorry for him. "He was scared to death," Leathers recalled. "He was just sitting there by himself at a desk scared to death."

Yet he looked forward to the challenge. "With two different shows a day," he told the *Southeast Missourian*, "I'll be getting two completely different sets of callers. I think that will keep me and the show spontaneous . . . I would rather do two shows than one longer one." Over time, as the demands of two shows intensified, he began to resent doing the local one. After all, he had gone to New York to reach the whole nation, not a bunch of rude New Yorkers. He was after his people in the heartland who were waiting for a new spokesman.

Rush arrived in New York during one of the city's most insufferable heat waves, and he had only been in town for a few days when he first went on the air. But nobody could tell, at least not McLaughlin.

"Here's a guy who had been to New York only one other time in his life, and he did an incredible show," McLaughlin said. "I couldn't believe anyone could do a show that well, and particularly not sound like he had never been to New York City before." From the beginning, he said, Rush "tried to make the local show a bit more New Yorkish. We talked about what was in the papers, but the natural flow of his interests took it more into the national scene, which the local community didn't find difficult; it was just different enough. WABC said he was a hell of a talent, and local or national didn't matter." For the next few weeks, Rush worked the local show while McLaughlin got the satellite ready for the national program.

Finally, on August 1, 1988, less than five years after he had left the Royals—the lowest point of his life—Rush Limbaugh put on his headphones and started broadcasting to America. The EIB— Excellence in Broadcasting (fictitious, of course)— Network was born, and so were the sobs, giggles, coughs, snatches of song, and other vocal effects that have marked his unique delivery ever since. The show made its debut on fifty-six radio stations, and only a few were in high-profile cities; none, with the exception of New York, of course, were in the top ten markets. McLaughlin had convinced ABC to let him take over all of the affiliates that had already been signed up for the network's midday talk-radio format. In other words, the stations were just along for the ride.

But the number of outlets wasn't the point. Rush finally had the forum he had always treasured, and, as such, there were the normal pressures lurking in his subconcious. Was he really good enough to pull this off? Was he the real thing or a fraud? Would he wake up one day and be back in radio obscurity, promoting Kiwanis Club dinners and relay races from some lonely outpost in the middle of nowhere? Would he even be in radio?

In Sacramento, he was a big deal. In New York, he was nothing. "It was part of the realization," McLaughlin said, "that when you come to New

York, you are just like everyone else; one of the seven million. People were saying, 'Who is this new guy from Sacramento? What makes him think he can come here and be a big hit?' "

Yet, if he was scared, he tried awfully hard not to show it. "This has been the easiest move of my life," he told the *Bee* in August of 1988. "Even if it fell apart in six months, I haven't lost a thing. Even if it doesn't work, everyone will know who I am. It's destiny."

15

NOT IN THE BEGINNING. NOBODY KNEW WHO HE was, and his only destiny seemed to be failure. A general manager at WABC told Rush that a national talk show wouldn't work. Rush was so despondent that he wondered whether he had made the wrong decision. "I was a basket case," he told the *New York Times*. McLaughlin took over as Rush's cheerleader, pumping him up with daily ego infusions when he got down, which was quite frequent. "That was the toughest thing for both of us," McLaughlin acknowledged, "to get through the first year."

Yet, in New York, Rush was almost timid compared to the opposition. "If Sacramento thought I was outrageous or obnoxious," he told the *Bee*, "they should hear the two other conservative daytime guys on the ABC affiliate in New York. One asks whether light-skinned blacks are better than black-skinned blacks. The other challenges 'faggots.' I'm the baby of the three of us and I think my decency will win out in the end."

He also couldn't resist another stab at his Sacramento predecessor, who was also trying to carve out a national reputation. "Unlike Mort Downey," he added, "I don't need to have a gay nun on to get people to listen. I don't intend to become a zookeeper like him."

Rush appreciated the fact that he wasn't taken as seriously in New York as he was in Sacramento. "What I do is shtick, show business," he told the *Bee*. "In New York, they realize this . . . women in Sacramento took my feminist jokes seriously and thought I was a fat, sexist piglet. Men in the newsroom didn't like it when I called them 'flaming libs.' They gave me my own office, but it was clear to me that they wanted me out of the newsroom . . . Here in New York, they're not sitting around waiting to be offended. Because I'm not a star and receive no perceived preferential treatment, they accept and like me."

Over the years, Rush has claimed in numerous interviews that he instantly fell in love with New York City. He raved about the restaurants and the culture and not having to drive anywhere. He also appreciated his new anonymity. "He liked the fact that he could come and go without having people know who he was," Sullivan said.

But in an August 1988 interview with the *Bee*, Rush sounded anything but in love. "No sane person would look forward to living in this city," he said. "The climate, lack of open space, lack of service unless you bribe someone . . . all of it just makes me look forward to when I can work from wherever I want. To live here, you have to forget everything you ever knew about decency." The location, however, was secondary to the opportunity because, as usual, he immersed

himself in his work, reading every newspaper he
could find to be more prepared than anyone else.
"My impression was that the guy got up early,
went to work, buried himself in his work, and
came home," Sullivan said. "You could've lived
in Toledo."

As Rush was trying to make it in New York,
Michelle finally sold the house and came to join
him. The possibilities were endless. Here they
were, a young couple, a rising star in American
broadcasting and his gorgeous blonde wife.

They would be unstoppable. Think of the speeches, the functions, the parties. Donald and Ivana
Who? Now they would be a long way from Kansas
City and poverty, even from Sacramento and partial
prosperity. Rush had arrived in New York, guaran-
teed to make at least $150,000 per year. Granted,
in New York that could evaporate in a few trips
to Bloomingdale's. But still, there would be plenty
of dough to wine and dine, to see plays and attend
museums, to live it up.

Michelle couldn't wait to get there. On the surface, her marriage, which had experienced serious
trouble several years back, appeared to have recu-
perated. They had talked things over and now things
seemed better.

But Michelle, as she now admits, was living in
a world of illusion. Popp, who used the same hair
stylist as Michelle in Sacramento, kept running into
her in the weeks and months before she left for New
York. She noticed a definite mood swing. "I sensed
a separation of direction," Popp said. "It was almost

like a coldness that had settled over, a resignation. I didn't feel the closeness that was there before . . . everytime I saw her, the excitement wasn't there that was there the time before. It seemed to kind of wane . . . I used to warn her, 'Be careful, this is Sacramento, this is a lot different than New York. Be sure you look after Michelle.' "

The first bad omen didn't take long to show up. The moving van that carried many of their household goods and clothes didn't arrive on time. Soon the Limbaughs discovered that the driver had abandoned the vehicle somewhere in Kentucky. "In the meantime, Rush was freaking out," Michelle said. "He drove me crazy." Fortunately, they recovered their stuff with everything totally intact.

Too bad the same couldn't be said of their marriage. Almost immediately after Michelle joined her husband in New York, it became pretty obvious, at least to her, that all the old problem areas that had first emerged in Sacramento had not really gone away, after all.

"Moving to New York and not knowing anyone and just having each other really brought things into clear focus," Michelle said, "and when you have a relationship, you can be distracted by a lot of other things around you, your job, your finances, your friends, your responsibilities, and that's what made me think for a long time that things were okay . . . But in New York, I saw how we both looked at marriage, and what was in store for us, and how things had evolved since the first time I had thought about getting a divorce, and so I just couldn't see going on the way that it was."

If Rush didn't have enough time for her in Sacramento, well surely he wouldn't have enough time for her in New York, especially as he was trying to make the difficult transformation from the small-city stud to the national star. Their marriage wasn't supposed to wind up this way. "He had told me that when we get to New York, we're going to do this, and do that," Michelle said, "and then, when we got there, we really didn't do anything. I just felt kind of cooped up."

Michelle said that Rush has implied that she expected him to do everything with her, but "that's an exaggeration." Perhaps the most revealing example of their divergent interests came when Michelle asked Rush to escort her to a Robert Mapplethorpe exhibit at the Whitney Museum of American Art in Manhattan. "I really wanted to see it because I'm a little into photography, and I envy people who can utilize it as an art form," Michelle said. This was before Mapplethorpe became very controversial, and Rush, ironically, became one of his critics. (In fact, Rush has used him as an example of what absurdity he believes can pass as art these days.)

Rush asked Michelle if they could postpone going until the following weekend, and she agreed. Then when the next weekend came, he repeated his request for more time. This pattern continued until Rush finally confessed. "You know, I really don't want to go," he told Michelle. "You know I've forgotten how incompatible we really are."

To Rush, it was a throwaway remark, intended to kind of laugh off their differences in a disarming way, and get on with *his* agenda: Work, work, work.

To Michelle, it summarized the growing gap between them. "That was one of the things that made me start thinking [again] about getting a divorce," she said. It made her realize that nothing had essentially changed since she had first contemplated leaving him a few years earlier. She had only been in New York about a month, but that was plenty of time to find out this problem would never go away. Rush was Rush.

He, of course, tried to talk Michelle out of it. But she knew she was right, which didn't make it any easier. "It was probably one of the most difficult decisions I had to make," she said, "because it wasn't as though he was a wife beater. He's a good person, and every other day I would change my mind. I wouldn't talk to him about it. It was something I had to grapple with myself. It was very difficult, and I'd be on the phone to my best friend in Sacramento, and even my mother. It was really hard, but I think I did the right thing for both of us."

Another thing that bothered Michelle was that she was beginning to get the feeling that she was somehow excluded from Rush's inner circle. Other people seemed more worthy of his attention. "I would hear things while he was talking on the phone," Michelle said, "that I would rather have heard for the first time if he were talking to *me*."

Michelle, however, decided to stay in New York. Just because her love for Rush couldn't overcome their fundamental differences didn't mean she was prepared to sever her ties with this exciting new city. She also wanted some privacy. "I didn't want to have to go back and answer anybody's questions in Sacramento," she said, "because I felt that wasn't anybody's business."

Rush, generous to the end, even let her stay with him in his West Side apartment until she could find her own place. She finally moved out on Christmas weekend. "I hated to do this," she said, "but for me it was becoming uncomfortable." It was the first time Michelle had ever been on her own; she had moved from her parents' house right into Rush's apartment in the summer of 1982.

Michelle had also met another man. At first Rush assumed that was the reason for the breakup, but all it did was fire off another warning shot to Michelle that the romance with Rush had completely cooled off. She was alarmed that she could feel such an attraction to someone else. "It wasn't the first time I felt myself looking around," she said, "and it was because I wasn't getting what I wanted out of our marital relationship, and I don't believe it was either of our faults. We had different ideas of what we wanted out of marriage, and there was no way for both of us to get what we wanted."

Rich Allen said he and his wife received a letter from Michelle shortly after the breakup with Rush which indicated she already had another boyfriend, and that he was a "real jock type fellow, athletic, etc . . . When people first get into a relationship that's particularly sexual, they go wild about it for a while; I had the impression that she had just discovered sex." Allen was among the couple's friends who were stunned by the announcement from New York. Susie Rodriguez said she almost "drove off the road" when she found out.

But not everybody was surprised. "In Sacramento, she was away from home for the first time," Nathan said, "so she kind of clung to him. She went from the age of twenty-three to twenty-seven, and that's a big change to go from a little kid out of school to being a very attractive woman in a world that has a lot of opportunities for you as an individual. So why be an extension of somebody else, which is what she feared becoming. She had a life to live, too."

For Michelle, it was a matter of space. "I totally lost my identity when I was with him," she said, "and now you can ask my current husband, I *cling* to my identity." (Michelle met her future husband, Alex Wennerholm, in June of 1989. He was an account executive for a Long Island marketing research company, and now he works in the health food industry for a grocery store chain. They reside in Oakland, California.)

Soon after Michelle decided to file for divorce, if she had any thoughts of reconsidering, hearing about Rush's new life probably put them away forever. "He was informing me that he was starting to fly to this city and that city almost every weekend," she recalled, "and his schedule was really booking up for the next three months. He was telling me some of the people that he was meeting and were throwing parties for him, like John and Bo Derek, and Jonathan Winters and Peter Noone (from Herman's Hermits).

"To me, I was relieved not to have to deal with that. It's not that I would be intimidated by these people because I'm not that way, but I was relieved because it just didn't seem like the kind of world I would want to be involved in— a lot of superficiality, people that are hung up on their image because that's part of their profession because they have to be concerned about that. You have to watch what you say, and who are you seen with, and your appearance, and I don't like to be concerned about all that."

Michelle has few regrets these days. Rush opened up an exciting new world to her, which she ultimately decided to explore without him. Sure he dominated her and his needs almost always came first, but it was because of Rush that Michelle saw the beauty of northern California and the glamour of New York. It was because of Rush that she learned about politics, power, and what dreams could unfold for a simple guy from Cape Girardeau and a simple gal from Kansas City. It was not the life that she wanted—it was *his* life—but it was one that made her grow up very fast.

Children, however, were not part of that life. Michelle said she was just beginning to entertain the idea when the marriage fell apart. She comes from a large family, and had done a lot of baby-sitting for her older brother and sister's kids. The experience is not one she recalls fondly. "The kids just took advantage of me," she said, "and it was not a fun situation . . . they were awful to me, so I didn't even think about having kids of my own." She kept thinking that maybe in her thirties, she might want to bear the next Limbaugh; she was twenty-seven when she walked out.

When people asked Rush if he and Michelle were going to have any kids, he used to joke: "Well, let's see how she does with the dogs first." That became a running gag between the two lovers. "Then after a while," she said, "it became an even bigger joke and I said, 'I must be doing really well, cause now we have two dogs.' "

But this was no laughing matter. Rush, unlike his grandfather and father, was not destined to become a father in his twenties or thirties. There would be no Rush Hudson Limbaugh IV to sit by the radio, and carry *his* father's message to the next generation. Rush is forty-two now, and based on a 1993 interview in the *New York Times*, he may never pass on that legacy. "A lot of people say, 'Why don't you have children?' " he said, "and aside from the fact that there's this thing called a woman that you need, I haven't got to the point where it's something that seems like the next step I should take. It's not an active desire that I have. Now, maybe that's a result of not being in love. Who knows?"

Christmas 1988 came, and suddenly, Rush was all alone in his big West Side apartment. He still had his computer, and his beloved video equipment, and he still had the enormous responsibility of being as informed as anyone else on the planet, but just as when Roxy left him a decade earlier, he was again stranded without a companion, and it hurt. He had proven his father wrong by finding a woman and managing to support her without a conventional, traditionally high-paying profession. He could support her, but he couldn't make her happy.

Naturally, Rush didn't reveal his pain to his mother and brother, who were convinced he handled adversity with amazing poise and restraint. "Believe me, I tested him on it," said David Limbaugh. "I was trying to open him up, and I didn't feel any bitterness at all." His mother also made herself available, but Rush didn't give in. "He didn't cry on our shoulder," she said. "He never does." That job of comforting was left to his friends, some of whom had never seen him more shaken. "He wasn't happy about it [the breakup]," said Nathan, "but he also knew it was inevitable, that it had been coming for some time."

When Michelle filed for divorce, there were some in Rush's family who feared the worst. Millie Limbaugh said that Rush's father was concerned that Michelle was going to take him for everything he owned.

But Michelle Sixta was not brought up to be a gold digger. "I'm not hung up on the money," she said. Instead, Rush and Michelle parted amicably, and became officially divorced in December of 1989, seven years after their wedding at Royals Stadium. From then on, until Michelle left New York in 1992, they met periodically for dinner; they became friends and still keep in touch. The last time she saw Rush in New York, she returned one of his most valuable possessions, his Kansas City Royals championship ring from 1980. "I think he'll always care for her," said Michelle's ex–college suitemate, Suzy Bellony.

16

RUSH, HIS HEART BROKEN AGAIN, TURNED TO THE only love he had left—radio. This was one partner he was going to make certain would never abandon him. "Obviously, it crossed my mind," McLaughlin said. "What's this [the breakup] going to mean to him? But you wouldn't have known that it had occurred if you didn't have actual knowledge of it." Rush had worked too hard, suffered the humiliation of too many setbacks, incurred the doubts of his family for too many years, not to devote every ounce of energy he had to become the best talk show host in America. The odds were stacked against him but those are Rush Limbaugh's favorite odds, and the battle began.

It would be the kind of battle waged in the small cities of America, where conservatism flourished and the all-powerful Eastern media didn't dictate the daily agenda. It would be waged in places like South Bend, Indiana, home of the legendary Fighting Irish of Notre Dame, and the spot where Rush Limbaugh made his first big stand against those who wanted to shut him up. The question was: Could the town win one for him?

The affiliate in South Bend implied that, because

of the growing volume of irate callers who found Limbaugh deeply offensive, it might have to break away from EFM. Such reaction was becoming an all too familiar pattern for the network. Most of the small stations carrying Rush were not accustomed to the booming voice of a conservative comedian with his ability to outrage. Their listeners were folks uncomfortable with change. They were used to easygoing personalities; Rush was from another stratosphere. A number of stations complained they weren't sure they could hang on for much longer. We love Rush, they said. We *don't* love the negative calls.

Finally, enough was enough. South Bend made Rush furious, and he decided to fight back. "Rush said, 'If we don't do something now, we could just go down the tubes because we'll never get a chance,'" McLaughlin recalled. "And I think we had seen enough positive impact from other stations that we felt that we weren't going to take this anymore."

So Rush went on the air to tell his listeners about the negative reaction, and urged them to ask the South Bend station to give the show more time. Rise up against the liberal establishment, he urged. Rise up and make your voice count. He offered the analogy that people who purchase a car only call the dealer if they experience any trouble, not if they're satisfied. Well, he exhorted them, tell the bastards you're more than satisfied.

"I think we needed that more for ourselves than we did about the station itself," McLaughlin said. "We had to say, 'Dammit, we are good enough.'"

The South Bend station was besieged with calls from all over the nation demanding that the show stay on the air. The first major test of Rush's emerging popularity was a huge success. His loosely connected core of diehards had demonstrated their mettle. They were beginning to build a support network for their new hero, the right-wing populist for the nineties.

Another challenge for the Limbaugh-McLaughlin team was how to combat the overriding perception in the business that a national radio talk show simply couldn't work. Sometimes, Rush wondered whether anyone, even someone with talent loaned from God, could penetrate the close-minded mentality of program directors across the country. "We were hearing from a lot of people—local, local, local," McLaughlin said. Stations would tell him "we don't want a national show. We'll take it at nighttime, but we're not going to give up our midday, and take calls from all over the nation, because in Chicago, we don't care what anyone in Birmingham, Alabama, says."

But McLaughlin had seen other entertainment talents—Carson, Donahue, Oprah—thrive on the national scene, and he saw no reason why Rush, even if he was in radio, couldn't do the same. McLaughlin felt he had proof that affiliate program directors were misguided. He pointed to Rush's ratings for KFBK, which had signed on with the national show from the beginning. Most people in the business assumed that KFBK's ratings would go down because Rush would no longer be focusing only on Sacramento. But the ratings went up.

From the start, McLaughlin wasn't too concerned with the total number of radio stations signing up with Rush. He wanted the biggies. He had New York, and he wanted Los Angeles, Chicago, and Detroit. "I knew, from my experiences," he said, "that if I could get into the top twenty markets with a pretty good representation—fourteen or fifteen of the top twenty—we could make it. I also knew I had to get into Los Angeles."

In early 1989, Limbaugh replaced Geoff Edwards on KFI in Los Angeles, and now he could be heard on the power centers of both coasts. "Once I had New York and Los Angeles," he said, "I really felt we were okay." Detroit came aboard shortly afterward and now EFM had lined up three of the top ten markets. They would not look back. Eventually, Rush was able to stop doing the local show, and extend the national program to its present three hours.

Along the way, not surprisingly, Rush took a severe beating from the media. The first count against him was that he was too conservative. The second was that he was too arrogant. "We had some bad newspaper press, which I expected," McLaughlin noted. "We were warned by the manager in Detroit that the newspaper guy there was going to tear us apart. The writer was a liberal, and he would totally disagree with Rush; it had nothing to do with the quality of the program, or the approach."

But the media weren't supposed to gravitate to Rush; after all, it was the media which Rush needed desperately as a target for his daily diatribes. It was the media which annoyed so many of his supporters from Middle America and made them cling to someone like Rush, who represented *their* interests. If the media had universally endorsed Rush, he, in fact, might have lost some of his credibility.

Meanwhile, the far more important constituency—the people—were flocking to their new prophet in amazing numbers. EFM was attracting the biggies, and the smaller outlets. One by one, local stations jumped on the Limbaugh bandwagon— by July 1990, 244 had signed up to hear the Gospel According to Rush. With these kinds of figures, advertisers, naturally, were anxious to be promoted by him. But Rush, fresh from his huckster days in Sacramento, realized that his credibility was even more critical before a national audience and, therefore, was extremely selective in which products he would endorse. He had to believe in them.

"My strategy was always, from day one, that we would not be traditional in terms of our marketing," McLaughlin said. They went after advertisers for whom it would be easier to track definitive results and who would likely stick with the program for the duration. Among the ones who met those requirements were the weekly publication, the *Conservative Chronicle*, and the popular beverage, Snapple. According to the *Washington Times*, the *Chronicle* was getting an average of ninety subscription inquiries a day since advertising on the show. Now those are some results.

Typically, as was the case with Snapple, Rush would announce first that he liked a certain product and then EFM would go out and try to sign up the company to advertise. It usually worked. "We found our own advertisers," Limbaugh told *Success Magazine*, "people who'd never been in radio before, and we made them gazillions." In 1992, some more traditional clients—AT&T and Motel 6—came aboard to make their own gazillions.

With his first year behind him, and the danger of imminent failure no longer on his mind, Rush went into cruise control. He told friends he was having "an adult Christmas every day." He hammered away at his standard liberal-bashing updates with the irreverence and sarcasm that program directors had, until Sacramento, always managed to stifle. He was nominated Personality of the Year in 1989 by the National Association of Broadcasters. McLaughlin was ready to appoint him God. Nobody would dare stifle him.

The updates were a huge hit. They included: the Animal Rights Update, in which Rush would reveal the latest grievance from animal rights activists, accompanied by Andy Williams singing "Born Free" to shouts of "Pull!", shotgun blasts and squealing animals; the Ted Kennedy Update ("I'm the type of guy who likes to roam around . . . I'm never in one place, I roam from town to town . . . "); the Sexual Harrassment Update, set to Frankie Valli's "My Eyes Adored You"; and the Homeless Update, in which the theme song was Clarence "Frogman" Henry's "Ain't Got No Home." Here, Rush's favorite target was homeless advocate Mitch Synder, who he felt grossly overexaggerated the magnitude of the problem. When Snyder committed suicide and a note was found, Rush, never the most sensitive observer, joked: "I wonder if I was mentioned."

One update got him in real trouble, and the out-raged were again members of the gay community. Rush had introduced the AIDS Update, with the theme songs: "I'll Never Love This Way Again" by Dionne Warwick or "Back in the Saddle Again" by Gene Autry. Homosexuals were furious that Rush poked fun at a disease that killed people. (Earlier, according to one newspaper account, he had called AIDS a "modern-day plague on homo-sexuals.")

Ultimately, he admitted his mistake, and pulled the AIDS updates after only a few weeks. "It's the single most regretful thing I've ever done," he told the *New York Times*, "because it ended up making fun of people who were dying long, painful, and excruciating deaths, when they were not the target. It was a totally irresponsible thing to do."

McLaughlin said Rush was particularly affected by the plight of actor/director Paul Michael Glaser ("Starsky and Hutch"), his wife, Elizabeth, and their children. Elizabeth had contracted the virus by way of a tainted blood transfusion in childbirth. Her baby got the virus and died. She and another child are HIV positive. Elizabeth established the Pediatric AIDS Foundation, and spoke about the disease at the 1992 Democratic Convention in New York.

Soon after Rush initiated the AIDS updates, McLaughlin met with members of the gay com-munity, and realized the disease was no longer strictly a homosexual problem. Rush had regis-tered complaints with the agenda and politics of the gay community, but not with the disease. "That touched him that children could get it, without any involvement in life except being unlucky through a bad blood transfusion," McLaughlin said.

The other major controversy of Rush's first two years on the national show was his legendary "caller abortions." Rush, a fierce pro-life advocate, had been talking about condoms on his show—it was Valentine's Day 1989—when a woman called in to talk about abortion. It was a total non sequitur, which completely irritated Rush, and he didn't know how to get rid of her. Hanging up was not an option, as he wanted to maintain his self-appointed title of America's "most polite talk show host"; this was quite ironic, incidentally, considering Rush had been the master of rudeness at KUDL's gripe line in the late 1970s. But this was the kinder and gentler Rush.

With the woman still on the line, Rush, according to his book, made a casual off-air comment to his call screener, saying he wished he could abort the call. Bingo, the caller abortion idea was born! His assistant, Phil Latzman, put together a twelve-second sound of a vacuum cleaner turning on, doing its thing, and then switching off, and mixed that with a seven-second tape of a scream. Rush estimates that he did about twenty caller abortion calls in two weeks.

But there was intense public reaction, which, according to Rush, even forced the cancellation of one station in Seattle. Rush felt the callers were not his regular listeners, but, in actuality, were abortion activists who viewed the controversy as a great opportunity to try to bring him down. His friends were sympathetic, as well. "He realized the caller abortions were distasteful," Nathan admitted, "but not everything in entertainment is tasteful and his stated objective from the get-go, as it should have been, is to build the largest audience you can."

Finally, however, in a rare capitulation to public opinion, Rush took the caller abortions off the program. In McLaughlin's view, the problem was that people didn't understand what Rush was trying to do, which was to alert people to the horror and immorality of an actual abortion. Instead, people felt offended and hurt by the screaming. "We realized that if they didn't understand it," McLaughlin said, "they might find it offensive, and then we'd never have enough time to tell them why it was being done." He said it played well in Sacramento because people there understood what Rush was doing. McLaughlin and Rush believe it takes a solid six weeks to get the full gist of what Rush is all about. Otherwise, anything a listener hears is usually way out of context.

As 1989 progressed, it became once again clear, just as it had in Sacramento, that the radio was too small to bottle up all the ambitions of Rush Limbaugh. It was time again to take his act on the road. At KFBK, Rush had been constantly requested as a speaker in northern California. Now, the whole nation would get a chance to hear what he had to say. Essentially, he would elaborate on the same general themes he espoused on his radio show: the problem is Washington, the problem is the liberal, the problem is the erosion of family values, the problem isn't you, the hard-working American. The problem is *them*.

Showing up in his limo, his tux, and with all the bravado only he could muster, Rush arrived in these towns as the conservative's Elvis, the rock star for people who don't follow rock stars. When he bounced onto the stage, they screamed. They loved it when he made fun of every conservative's favorite target—Ted Kennedy. (During the debate over the nomination of Supreme Court Justice David Souter, according to *Time* magazine, when an opponent hypothesized that the nominee was "in the closet," Rush said: "I think any of us would be safer in a closet with Judge Souter than we would be in an automobile with Ted Kennedy.")

They loved it when he made fun of the environmentalists, the feminists, the animal rights activists. Pick a liberal, and he trashed them. The crowd lost it when Rush broke into funny voices, such as squeaky dolphin talk or falsetto sobbing to mock bleeding hearts, or when he propelled his bulging figure into comical positions or imitated an environmentalist skipping through the woods.

The shows were part college lecture, part stand-up comedy, and part vaudeville. They were Las Vegas. And they made Rush a very happy and successful man.

According to one newspaper account, Rush earned $8,000 per show, and a video of his first tour netted him $80,000. Call it "Rush to Riches." Several thousand would attend each performance, at anywhere from $15 to $50 a crack for about ninety minutes of nonstop entertainment. It was quite a Rush.

Rush, the consummate businessman, took home a significant percentage of the profits. "When we opened the tickets for sale at Bally's in Reno," recalled Jim Barnes, who put the show together and produced videos of his appearances, "they had a line out the door. That hadn't happened for anybody else." The stage was special to Rush. "It's the only way I have complete control of my image," he told the *Bee*. "When I'm going by the radio station, when I'm doing the interview at the newspaper, my image is controlled largely by the conditions. But on stage, it's all in my control. On stage, nobody can hand me a note about the pinto-bean dinner."

17

During one "Rush To Excellence" stop, he came back to Sacramento's Arco Arena, where thousands of screaming fans awaited the return of their adopted son. He was no longer, however, just the talk show host who owned Sacramento; he was after a nation now. As such, he had the age-old prerogative of power—an entourage. An entourage takes care of things, from taking suits to the dry cleaners to taking trespassers to the cops. An entourage means one has arrived.

One of his staff's duties was to make sure everything was prepared for his speaking engagements. Barnes took care of the Arco Arena visit, and thought it would be an interesting twist to ask Rush's ideological opposite, Christine Craft, to introduce him. Craft, who had filed a celebrated lawsuit in the 1980s against a company that owned a Kansas City television station that had demoted her for being too old and not being deferential to men, and had gotten along with Rush when he worked at KFBK, consented in a second. "I thought it would be a kick," she said. "I knew I'd be going into an audience of six-thousand fascist reactionary conservatives . . . This was his crowd, not mine, but I thought it would be funny."

But Rush's handlers thought it might be too funny. Craft, they feared, might plan some kind of demonstration to embarrass Rush and his cohorts. So it was time to implement damage control, but Christine Craft was not going to be a willing participant. She received a phone call one day from one of Rush's assistants who asked to see a copy of her script. As a journalist and strong proponent of the First Amendment, Craft refused to hand it over. Worse, she refused to even talk to Limbaugh. "That blew them away," she said, "that someone would deny the opportunity to talk to Rush Limbaugh."

She also threatened to pass entirely on the introduction and force the show's sponsors to find a replacement at the last minute if they kept insisting on seeing the script. They finally backed off. "I was very offended," she said. "I was named one of the five best collegiate speakers in the country when I was on a lecture tour. Speaking extemporaneously is not a right reserved for Rush Limbaugh or anybody, for that matter."

She went ahead with the introduction, which, she said, was anything but a vicious attack on Rush. Craft claims it was funny, and charming, and won over many in the enemy camp who were poised to boo her all the way to Palo Alto. She gave a Nelson Mandela shirt to Rush, as well as the tail feather of a spotted owl—the owl was a favorite Rush target—and a Ken doll wearing a tutu to help him understand the changing gender roles in modern society. This was the kind of stuff Rush would pull.

To Craft, however, the whole incident was the

perfect example of what can happen to a nice guy when he gets intoxicated by a little power. "I felt there was a real turning point in who he had become," Craft said. "He was surrounded by people who were telling him things he chose to believe. The very fact that he'd try to censor someone else who does the same thing he does speaks volumes about how much class some-one has . . . the gracious person I knew in the newsroom was no more. He had gotten so full of himself that he gave no one else any quarter."

Craft said Rush never bothered to register his appreciation for her introduction, or to even offer an apology. "I thought maybe he'd drop a little note saying, 'Thanks, I was wrong,' something to admit that censorship, something he'd never tolerate for himself, is not something you should try to put on other people."

Barnes, the general manager at Filco, a seven-chain appliance company that was one of Rush's biggest advertisers in Sacramento, never thought an apology was necessary. "She didn't tell anyone what she was going to say," he said, "and we had tons of money invested." Barnes said when he originally posed the idea of the introduction to her, it was not a formal invitation. The next thing he knew, she was accepting the offer on the air. Filco was stuck with her.

Rush and Craft became rivals, and hooked up in another major dispute. Rush was asked to produce a daily front-page column for the *Sacramento Union*, the conservative alternative to the *Bee*. It gave him a platform to attack the same left-wing targets he maligned on the radio. It also gave him an extra aura of legitimacy; he was, in a way, becoming a part of the press, mainstream or not. But Craft, a new Limbaugh watchdog, told her listeners that Rush did not write the column. She could tell because it was so poorly written. "The latest Milli Vanilli is right here in Sacramento," she announced on her show.

Rush went crazy, and went on the attack. "This is absurd and a waste of time," he said, through a spokesman, to *Editor & Publisher* magazine. "The column is transcribed by a Union editor from my daily radio program. It is just like dictation, except that the transcription is faxed to me whereupon I retool it for written form, then submit it to the paper for publication. Any suggestions to the contrary are unfounded, uninformed and unprofessional."

But Dan Vierria, the *Bee's* television and radio columnist, reported, according to *Editor & Publisher*, that Rush had told him that he edits (not writes) the column, saying, "What difference does it make? It's hot, it's honest and it doesn't threaten America."

To Craft, it makes a huge difference. "Someone might think that's a little thing," she said, "but I'm a writer. I've written books by myself and I've written columns for various papers, and I've always written them by myself. If you write it, you write it. If you don't, you don't claim that you do. It has to do with integrity. It's fraudulent." Regarding Rush's counterattack against her: "I'm not the one who is passing something off as a column when it isn't."

But the conflicts with Craft were contained and manageable, and few people outside Sacramento ever found out about them. Rush would not, however, be so fortunate with every dispute. In the late winter of 1990, Rush was asked by Rod Perth, vice president of late-night entertainment at CBS, to host "The Pat Sajak Show" for one night. Sajak was sinking in the ratings, and CBS, fearing it would lose the hour back to its affiliates, was searching the nation for a talk show host to excite the next generation. Perth thought Rush might be that guy. "He was incredibly effective in another medium," Perth said. "He was part of a rather diverse list."

Talk about legitimacy; you can't get much more credibility than CBS and late-night television. It was a tremendous opportunity for an artist who still had one medium left to conquer.

Yet it was also a tremendous trap. Rush, after all, was no Garry Shandling, no safe, middle-of-the-road veteran who could soothe a country going to sleep. He came to CBS with a lot of baggage, and television networks don't like baggage because most Americans don't like baggage. But they felt he could pull in a lot of his radio audience, and show the affiliates that CBS was serious about replacing Sajak with a better product. Besides, he had been a guest on the show before and was very well received.

CBS saw his appearance as an unofficial audition. If he could score here, maybe he'd get his own late-night show. This fact, of course, did not escape the ever-ambitious Rush. "Television is something I'm trying to learn," he told the *Los Angeles Times*. "You never know where these things lead."

The baggage had to do with his gay problem. Rush, just three months earlier, had, according to newspaper accounts, affirmed his antigay reputation by lashing out at AIDS activists who disrupted services at St. Patrick's Cathedral in New York, commenting: "I say to those of you of the leftist, militant, homosexual crowd: Take it somewhere else. Get out of our schools. Get out of our churches. Take your deadly, sickly behavior and keep it to yourselves." Rush insisted that his anger was aimed at the hard-core activists, and not the general gay population. "I'm a political enemy of theirs," he told *Newsday*. "Yet they call me a homophobe. But I'm not."

That disclaimer did nothing to make him any more acceptable. "His audience does not make a distinction between gay and lesbian activists and the gay community," Zane Blaney, media committee chairman of San Francisco's GLAAD (Gay and Lesbian Alliance Against Defamation) told *Newsday*. "And he doesn't either. I don't believe he does all this in an angelic frame of mind."

Yet Rush was determined not to incite that kind of controversy on television. TV is, after all, a cold medium; radio is red hot. TV is supposed to be polite; radio is a town hall meeting where everyone is expected to be obnoxious. "On radio, you can be a little controversial," he told the *Los Angeles Times*. "You can come back the next day and explain what you mean to people who don't get it. On a one-shot television show, you have to, in my mind, start out at a pace where you just don't totally blow people away." What made Rush's behavior even more critical was that CBS had just dealt with the Andy Rooney affair. Rooney, the popular humorist on "60 Minutes," had been suspended for making derogatory comments to a gay publication. Would Rush be Rooney II?

He didn't get a chance. On March 30, shortly after he started his monologue with typical arrogance, "I'm here to save CBS," members of an AIDS-activist group, ACT-UP, shouted: "Go home!" and "You're a Nazi." CBS first tried to identify the protesters, but it was impossible because they kept moving from seat to seat. Finally, the whole audience was cleared before Rush could resume. An hour show took more than three hours to tape. Rush desperately wanted to retaliate, but he knew this was not the right time. One ill-conceived outburst, and the entire show might have been scrapped, and he might never make it back on network television. "They weren't interested in talking," said Rush to *Newsday*, referring to the protesters. "All they wanted to do to me was shut me up." Either way, the show was a disaster and Rush could forget about his own series.

"It was a horrible night," recalled Perth. "He came out full of bluster and left a very shaken man. He was a mess. I had never seen a man sweat as much in my life." Yet, amid the rubble of one of the worst nights of his career, Rush demonstrated a glimpse of what the future might be. "It certainly convinced me he wasn't the answer for CBS," Perth said, "but I saw a genuine warmth and an ability to communicate . . . We had a hand-held camera as he walked down the hallway with the Mayflower Madam [Sydney Biddle Barrows, a guest on the show] and he was engaging. There was an obvious connection with the camera."

His other early ventures into television also didn't get anywhere. There was talk of a call-in show for CNN, à la Larry King, but, according to Rush, a network executive told him: "Everybody here loves your tape. They just wish you were a little more liberal." He also auditioned for the remake of "To Tell the Truth," whose producer, Mimi O'Brien, wasn't concerned with his ideological leanings. He was one of twenty people considered as a panelist. "He's bright, articulate, intelligent," O'Brien told the *Los Angeles Times*. But he wasn't hired.

Another possible television vehicle for Rush was a pilot he did with Gloria Allred, tentatively entitled, "Talk Wrestling." In it, the two of them debated the prominent issues of the day, engaging in the standard kind of sarcasm and ridicule that would make for great entertainment. Allred certainly gave as good as she got. "I didn't get the feeling that he liked confrontation with me," Allred said. "I think Rush prefers to be Rush." Unfortunately, Rush never got the opportunity to be Rush and tackle Allred on a regular basis. The pilot wasn't picked up. Jim Paratore, senior vice president of Lorimar Telepictures, which developed the show, said Rush displayed instant magnetism.

"He was very comfortable in front of the camera," Paratore said. "We always felt there was something there. We liked him, but we weren't sure whether he could do it all alone." By the time Paratore thought of exploring another television vehicle for Limbaugh, the radio host was too busy in New York. For Rush, not landing on television was a setback, but hardly one that haunted him. He knew he'd be back.

"I've yet to have any fun doing a television show," he told the *Washington Times*. "I don't think TV knows what to do with me."

Yet his passion for that podium was not going to go away. "I'd like to be a comedian and I don't mind being a serious talk-show host," he told the *Los Angeles Times*. "I want to do both. And I think it can be done. I think there's a market for it."

18

ONE MARKET AT A TIME. RADIO WAS STILL THE place where the Limbaugh Legend was making its way from town to town. He was so lavished with compliments, in fact, that it started to break up the flow of his show. He was becoming tired of fans wasting valuable time that could be better used to spread more of his conservative ideas. One day, a caller remarked "ditto" to a previous fan's praise, and the term was forever enshrined. Callers regularly began merely to say "ditto," and the rest was understood. Rush lovers became known as "dittoheads." "Now every stadium we go to," his old pal, George Brett, said, "I hear, 'Hey, I'm a dittohead.' It's weird."

Even McLaughlin had to admit that the show was growing far beyond his original expectations. McLaughlin, a goal-oriented kind of guy, had hoped that Rush would reach 350 affiliates within five years, or August of 1993. That was his best-case scenario drawn from the fact that 350 AM stations in the country operated in the talk-radio format when Rush first started. A more immediate goal was 250 stations for the first three years.

Rush surpassed all of those forecasts. His numbers were incredible. March 1989: 110 stations. August 1990: 250 stations. October 1990: 280 stations. February 1991: 300 stations. April 1992: 465 stations. October 1992: 529 stations. McLaughlin's goal was achieved within just *three* years. By 1993, Rush had gone from 56 stations to ten times that number. The show was so successful that advertising rates went up to nearly $6,000 per 30-second spot. In his prediction, McLaughlin hadn't counted on the fact Rush would also attract stations which operated under different formats, but were willing to break the mold for a few hours each day specifically to sign up with EFM. Rush revolutionized radio.

"There must be 200 radio stations that are still on the air because of Rush," said Randall Bloomquist, news and talk editor of *Radio and Records* magazine, in an interview with *Success*. "If he were to get hit by a bus tomorrow, they might go off the air." WWL in New Orleans, for example, according to *Vanity Fair*, leapt from seventh to first in its time period when it signed up with Rush.

The success was so startling that McLaughlin eventually renegotiated Rush's contract, telling one publication it was "one of the most lucrative that's ever been written," although it would not move Limbaugh ahead of Paul Harvey as radio's highest-paid personality. "If a guy hits .400 and he has two years left on his contract," said McLaughlin, "I think you ought to renegotiate his contract." McLaughlin had good reason. According to *Success*, Rush brought EFM revenues up from $600,000 in 1989 to $1.2 million in 1990, $2.4 million in 1991, and $3.5 million in 1992.

McLaughlin wouldn't reveal the exact dollar figures, but did acknowledge the contract would take the show through the end of the century. Rush, as an equity partner in EFM, would continue to share in the program's profits. "I've always believed," McLaughlin said, "that the personality on the air is more than that. He's also the executive producer and does a lot more work than being on the air in contributing to the success of the program. Therefore, they should participate in the results."

As Rush's popularity skyrocketed, so did his bank account. He reportedly went from earning several hundred thousand dollars a year in 1989 to nearly a million in 1990 to $1.7 million in 1991, which counted his personal appearances—up to $25,000 a crack—on the "Rush To Excellence" tour, plus other speaking engagements and merchandise sales.

No single event proved to McLaughlin that Rush's show was going to be the sensation that it became. It was a combination of factors: the numbers, obviously, the fiercely loyal comments from his fans, and the huge profits of advertisers. Then, in 1989, McLaughlin escorted Limbaugh and his fans on a week-long cruise to the Caribbean. About 550 paid $1,500 apiece to hear Rush preside at two roundtable discussions and one auditorium performance. He also provided some ad hoc entertainment, such as shouting insults at Fidel Castro as their boat sailed close to Cuba. He just couldn't resist.

"We sold out that boat much faster than anyone had ever done," McLaughlin said. "I met with the people on that boat, and it gave me a real sense of his connection with those people. They came from all walks of life, from all parts of the country. And I saw that here was someone saying something that a lot of people believed in."

Take the homeless, for example. A lot of people believed Rush when he said the homeless are pampered too much by government programs, and should be taught more about how to lift themselves out of their permanent cycle of dependence. With Mitch Snyder dead, Rush needed another convenient symbol for his displeasure on this issue. Actor Martin Sheen was the obvious choice.

Sheen, as honorary mayor of Malibu, California, had declared the city a sanctuary for the dispossessed. Limbaugh promptly announced to his listeners that he was making buses available to transport the homeless from anywhere in the country to Malibu. He said he would hold a contest to see which of the cities that carried his show would charter the first bus of "indigents and illegal aliens" to the "left coast." Once again, Rush was perceived as insensitive to a very serious problem in America. Sheen, without naming Rush but the implication was unmistakable, condemned "irresponsible media personalities who have abused their power to gain ratings by treading on misery and suffering."

And, once again, Rush had gone too far. Fortunately, the penalty, since he was now such a major figure, was an apology or a withdrawal; in the old days, it usually meant he would soon be out of work. "I made a real blunder there," he admitted to the *Los Angeles Times*. "I don't exploit the homeless. I wanted to discredit Sheen."

That didn't stop him, however, from continuing to mock the homeless. "One of the things I want to do before I die," he told a packed audience in Irvine, California, according to the *Times*, "is conduct the homeless Olympics." He said events would include: "the ten-meter Shopping Cart Relay, the Dumpster Dig and the Hop, Skip and Trip." The audience erupted in laughter and applause. The homeless could always be counted on for a good laugh.

Occasionally, though, controversy would come running to Rush. In 1991, when Vincent Blades, a twenty-four-year-old homosexual, was murdered in Sacramento, Limbaugh's old nemesis, the Rev. Jerry Sloan, spoke at the memorial service and accused "Rush 'I never met a gerbil I didn't like' Limbaugh" of murder because his antigay rhetoric was responsible for the hatred many in society feel toward gays. Two years later, Sloan stands by his position. "He's a scumbag," Sloan said.

Rush defended himself in normally irreverent fashion. "On my radio show I initially volunteered to fly back to the region at my own expense (without the necessity of formal extradition)," he wrote in his *Sacramento Union* column, "offer myself for questioning and submit to rigorous interviews by law enforcement officers. I further agreed to be strip searched and whipped if necessary to make me responsive. I even offered to sit under that blaring interview light and be badgered mercilessly."

On a more serious note, Rush said Sloan's accusation is "illustrative of a theme which underlies the thinking of the militant homosexual community today. People are not to be held responsible for their own behavior. If any negative consequences flow from their misconduct, it is not their fault, but that of someone else. Until the true murderer is apprehended, I guess I will remain a suspect." He couldn't resist one final attempt at humor: "Maybe I should call Daryl Gates [embattled Los Angeles police chief, who was dealing with the fallout from the Rodney King beating] and ask him to recommend a lawyer." The *Sacramento Union*, of course, backed Rush all the way. "That kind of hateful and inciting talk does nothing to heal this community," it said in an editorial. "It will only encourage a new cycle of violence."

These conflicts, however, were mere sideshows to the Main Event: the Recognition of Rush. One media outfit after another was coming to terms with this new prince of the airwaves, who was the most important figure in the medium since Arthur Godfrey in the 1950s. *Newsweek*, *Time*, *Vanity Fair*, *People*, the *New York Times*, and "60 Minutes" all stepped forward with their dissection of the man and what he meant to American society. Rush was able to receive the legitimacy he had long craved without compromising an inch in his distrust of the liberal Establishment and the newspapers that perpetuate its positions.

Unlike some early stories, which were predominantly bash Rush pieces, the second round of coverage was much more complimentary. The *New York Times Magazine* story, for example, written by Lewis Grossberger, entitled, "The Rush Hours," which came out in December of 1990, symbolized the general shift. "That was an excellent article,"

McLaughlin said. "I think the fella who wrote that piece was the first one who approached it totally differently than anybody else. He spent a week with Rush, and really understood what he was writing about. It got to the essence of the man."

Other publications followed suit, including *Vanity Fair*, which provided the first hip story about Rush: "Describing Limbaugh as the hottest talk show host on the air only hints at the phenomenon. More significant, there is nothing else like him."

Time magazine was next: "The comet of Limbaugh's rise is the traditional American success story, rewritten for the Reagan-Bush era." On and on it went, and it hasn't stopped since.

19

Through it all, Rush's War against Women never had a cease fire. Hostilities had started when he came up with the disparaging phrase, "feminazis," and continued with his stance against abortion and his constant pokes at PMS (Pre-Menstrual Syndrome). Rush suggested that because PMS turns a woman into "a hellion," the U.S. Army should, on any given week of the year, prepare a "combat-ready battalion of Amazons to go into battle. Imagine that you are Manuel Antonio Noriega. You are in the Papal Nuncio in Panama City. You feel safe. All of a sudden, you hear this bloodcurdling scream outside. 'I am outraged!' And there is Sgt. Major Molly Yard [then head of NOW], leading a battalion of Amazons with PMS over the hill! That would be enough to scare the pants off anybody."

In the summer of 1991, Rush was given an even better target, and it was one that mobilized many women to hate him all over again. Enter stage left, Anita Hill.

From the beginning, Rush said he believed Hill was lying about the sexual advances of Supreme Court Justice nominee Clarence Thomas. He considered the whole affair a savage attack against an honorable man. "I think she has been [in love] with him for a long time," Rush said on the air, "and I think he spurned her. I think it's get-even time . . . Feminists are saying sexual harassment is now the plague of America and all men are guilty of it. I feel almost as if this has happened to me."

Many other public figures, of course, believed Hill wasn't telling the truth, but Rush had the clout to give it significant weight. Women perceived his stand as another case of Rush appealing to his core audience—middle-class, middle-aged white guys who don't know how to deal with the female of the 1990s. The Arbitron ratings provide further evidence: Rush does extremely well with women, but his strongest audience is, by far, men. For people twenty-five to fifty-four, for example, in some areas, approximately three times as many men as women listen to Rush.

"He does extraordinarily well with men," KFBK's Rich Eytcheson told the *Bee*. "Rush and I are almost exactly the same age. Although I may not agree with him politically, I share his confusion with how to deal with the changing role of the middle-aged white male. Rush is particularly good at verbalizing that confusion."

Rush has always been a sexist. In 1990, he began requiring that women listeners send him photos before he would take their calls. His office, according to the *Washington Times*, was bombarded with pictures, including nude photos and one snapshot of an elderly female listener holding an assault rifle. It was inscribed, "Earth First, go ahead and make my day," a reference to the activist environmental group.

He defended the requirement as a harmless attempt to get more women listeners—they are traditionally less likely to call radio talk shows—to participate. But his critics said such stunts were insensitive and demeaned women. Nor did comments such as: "I like the women's movement . . . from behind" help his image. Or maybe they helped it enormously.

In another example, during an appearance in 1992 on CBS "This Morning," the network, according to *Vanity Fair*, showed a clip in which Limbaugh told a story about a group of women who had won admission into an exclusive, all-male club and then demanded their own exercise room. The response from the membership, according to Rush, was: " 'We'll be glad to give you your own exercise room; in fact, we'll even put the first three pieces of exercise equipment in there for you. They put in a washing machine, ironing board, vacuum cleaner." Co-anchor Harry Smith laughed but his colleague, Paula Zahn, did not.

There are countless other examples. At KMBZ in Kansas City, Rush consistently referred to the news anchor as "the lovely and gracious Mary McKenna." Others became disturbed by such a sexist and unprofessional introduction, and eventually McKenna persuaded him to drop it. "He went into some dissertation about how Mrs. Kaufman, the wife of the owner of Royals Stadium," McKenna said, "was always introduced as the 'lovely and gracious Mrs. K.' . . . he made some type of comparison . . . Rush felt he put women on a pedestal. That it is why he said what he did."

Closer to home, Rush, since his divorce to Michelle, has not exactly turned into the reincarnation of Don Juan. He dates, but a third marriage seems a long way off, if ever. He is far too consumed by his work to have enough time to devote to anybody else. It was always the truth. Now, he admits it.

But others who have remained in touch with Rush believe that, despite all the professional triumphs he has attained, he is still a lonely, middle-aged guy looking for someone to understand him. In late 1991, Popp, his old Sacramento rival, interviewed him and found a more vulnerable Rush. The guy who had been committed to at least trying to lose weight had let himself become a blimp after Michelle left. Why bother anymore?

"I got the feeling that he's a little lonely," said Popp, "and I don't know if he'll ever find someone to fill that void. He's at a point where there's that trust issue. Are they [the women] there because he's Rush Limbaugh or do they really care about him? Michelle did, because she was with him in the beginning, when it was just Rush Limbaugh, the guy. That love, that devotion, I don't know if he'll ever find that. Even though it didn't work this time around, he still needs that.

"Looking at his own attitudes and life-style, he feels he had grown so selfish in the past couple of years that he doesn't know if anyone would tolerate him. He told me that he dates occasionally, and that he is an incurable romantic, but he finds it difficult to express it." (One of Rush's favorite movies of all time is *Love Story*. "I loved the ending," he said.)

In many ways Rush is at the same place with women as he was in Cape Girardeau. "I think it's something to do with my weight," he told *Vanity Fair*, "something to do with my memories of high school and so forth." "When I hear that women are interested in me, I don't believe it." Popp asked him about his vision of the perfect woman, and was shocked at the reply. "He said it would be someone who is totally self-sufficient, and doesn't feel they need him as a form of entertainment," Popp said. Rush was describing a feminist, and he knew it.

"I'm sure he wants to be married," added Tom Hazlett, a good friend from Sacramento, "and to someone who really appreciates his work and really likes talking politics, because I know Michelle wasn't into that. She wasn't real independent. When he sat around and played on the computer at night, she needed something to do, and it wasn't a lot of fun for her."

Others think Rush will find a woman in the past, not present. "He's gun shy," said Millie Limbaugh. "I'm sure he worries about his judgment. You wouldn't believe the letters I get from these women sending pictures. They think they'd be perfect for him. Anybody who would do that, you don't want them. I hope he finds someone. Every man needs a good woman . . . He'd make a wonderful husband, but he's going to have to find a girl that's a lot like we used to be, the good-old girl."

Rush continues to date, and was linked last year to Donna Dees, CBS spokesperson for Dan

Rather. Dees is proof of another cardinal Rush rule: It's okay to mix politics and romance. "I have lots of friends who are liberal, commie bastards," Limbaugh said with a smile to *USA Today*. "I don't form friendships based on ideological opinions. I'm not a judgmental person."

While vehemently disagreeing with his politics, Dees finds Rush "kind of sweet, and charming, and he's a good listener . . . After we argued one evening over Clarence Thomas," she told *USA Today*, "he sent me flowers and a card that said 'Anita Hill is not a liar. I'm trying. Rush.' While I know he didn't really mean it, the gesture was far more romantic and creative than any of the lies I've heard from the politically correct men I know." Dees believes the popular perception of her boyfriend is way too slanted. "He is not the Anti-christ that my feminist friends painted him as," she told *Time*. Listening to his show, she claims, "I haven't been that offended. Actually, I think he's kind of funny."

20

IN 1989, PERHAPS EVEN MORE IMPORTANT THAN ALL the accolades from his adoring fans—megadittos from Missoula, Montana, etc.—Rush found his way into the household that mattered the most. KZIM in Cape Girardeau signed up with EFM, and now, eighteen years after Rusty Sharpe left the air and graduated into the real world, much to the disgrace of his family, the Limbaugh voice was back where it belonged.

Finally, his father, who had heard the stories of Rush's success in Sacramento and New York and had read all the impressive news clippings, could find out for himself what his son had become. After all, he was the biggest skeptic of all, the one who warned Rush he would never be able to support a woman in such an unpredictable, unrespectable, low-paying profession. He was the one who finally felt relieved when Rush joined the Royals. And he was the one who felt crushed all over again when his son went back into radio. He was the one Rush wanted to impress. At first, he didn't do a good job. Rush, Jr., considered his son's shtick to be undignified and childish. Rush, Jr., always preferred serious conservative analysis to the kind of circus act Rush performed on the air. "My dad did not have the same type of sense of humor as my brother or my mom or I," said David Limbaugh, "and he was very serious-minded about politics. He felt my brother's audience was primarily a result of his political views and conservatism, and that Rush ought not to be too flippant . . . with these updates and all. My mom ate it up. My dad, I don't think, really understood it."

One appearance on national television changed all that. Ted Koppel invited Rush to be a guest in a "Nightline" discussion about the Persian Gulf War. Mark Shields of the *Washington Post* played the dove, Rush the hawk. For Rush, it was another symbol of acceptance; he wasn't just another loony radio guy idolized by middle-aged sexists in Middle America. He was a voice of authority that deserved a late-night forum. In Cape Girardeau, Rush's parents turned on the television and watched with tremendous pride. His father, who was hard of hearing, sat in amazement. "Where the hell does he get that from?" he said to his wife. The answer was obvious. "From you."

Rush probably became the proudest parent in town. In August of 1990, when their car finally surrendered to old age, and Rush, Jr., wasn't able to work, Rush bought his parents a new white Taurus. "Rush, Jr., and I went by his dad's house, and Pop came out to the car," Millie recalled, "and Rush, Jr., said, 'Dad, do you know of anyone else who has a son who could buy their father a car?' And Pop said, 'I sure don't.' . . . Before he died, he realized what was happening to Rusty, and just marveled at it."

David Limbaugh said his brother was happy to hear about his father's sudden new awareness of him. "When I told my brother [about the 'Nightline' comment], he was very gratified," David said. "Because we all, in my immediate family, did try to please my dad. We had so much respect for him and his intellect that it would be the ultimate triumph to have our dad think that we excelled in areas that he was good in, or that we were articulate about political or governmental issues."

In December 1990, Rush, Jr., died. He was seventy-two. He had contracted diabetes in the early 1960s and had never managed to control his weight. (Understandably, the family worries that Rush III will make the same mistake. Rush has tried numerous diets, and none of them have kept him slim for long.)

The death hit Rush very hard, although his brother was much more visibly upset. His father, in fact, was such a revered figure in Cape Girardeau that the *Southeast Missourian* devoted an entire editorial to his passing: "Rush's legendary fierceness as an advocate was so awe-inspiring that it marked him as a standout even in a family of distinguished attorneys."

On his show, Rush paid a moving tribute to his father, and warmly acknowledged his impact in his best-selling book, *The Way Things Ought To Be*. He is very grateful for what his father taught him. It was during those lectures in the living room, when the booming voice of an imposing father made him think about the world beyond high school, that

Rush Hudson Limbaugh III learned how to communicate. He studied under a pro.

But his father's strong presence was also a curse. So many decisions—going to college, marrying Roxy, leaving radio, etc.—had to be based on what Dad might think. Not that Rush wasn't willing to go against his father's wishes; he did that on many important occasions. But always in the distance, he knew his dad was watching, judging, and it affected him profoundly. He was never quite sure whether he'd get his approval, or if he'd ever match up to his father's greatness. He spent the first forty years of his life searching for that answer.

Mary Jane Popp thinks he is still searching. "And you know what? He'll never reach it," Popp said. "He is going to constantly want more and bigger and more and bigger and when he reaches that plateau, it ain't going to be enough . . . anything that he does will never be as good as his father, as good as persons with degrees, as good as, I don't know, what he wants to be as good as. He should be as good as Rush wants to be, but he's not comparing himself to himself. He's comparing himself to everyone else."

Yet Rush has managed to go places his father never could, like the White House, for example. For years, Rush, Jr., was very proud of a picture taken of him with President Nixon when he was running for vice president, but that was as close as he got to the pinnacle of power in America. His highest title was Republican County Chairman. His son, however, had more than a photo opportunity with a president; he *slept* in the Lincoln Room.

All this happened, of course, because of Rush's emerging importance in the 1992 presidential contest. George Bush was in deep trouble all year long, from the surprise of Pat Buchanan to the sideshow of Ross Perot to the stubbornness of Bill Clinton. To Bush, Rush was a ticket to the disenchanted middle-class taxpayers who threatened to give the country back to the Democrats. He knew he had to shore up his base from 1988, and stem the erosion that was occurring from state to state. Hence, George Bush was kowtowing to Rush Limbaugh, and Rush knew it.

"I was creaming President Bush," said Rush, who openly supported Buchanan during the primaries, to the *Chicago Tribune*, "because I wanted the conservative message in his campaign. I thought that was the only chance he had to win. I kept saying so during the presidential campaign, and when they were running a rotten campaign, I said so." The Bush people, understandably, were alarmed at Rush's attacks. He was causing serious damage.

In June, Bush invited Rush to his home. He went to the Kennedy Center with the president and Mrs. Bush. After his foray into culture—Michelle would have loved that—Rush returned to the White House, and spent the night in the Lincoln Room. At one point in the evening, Bush actually carried Limbaugh's overnight bag to the bedroom.

"The president never once asked me about the views of my listeners," Rush said in a written statement to the *Washington Post*. "He did, however, ask me for my views on a few things." And there it was: Rush Limbaugh, the failure of his own family, was being asked for his opinions by the president of the United States. Rush told reporters that later that night, Bush showed him a video of "Saturday Night Live" comedian Dana Carvey doing an impression of Ross Perot. Then, Rush did a Perot imitation, and the president laughed. It was a wonderful evening.

A few months later, in early October, Rush even broke one of his most cherished rules to honor his new friend. George Bush was allowed to be a guest on Rush's show, one of the rare visitors Rush has allowed since he went national in 1988. (The others had included Pat Buchanan, former Education Secretary Bill Bennett, and Col. Oliver North. Usually, these Rush favorites called him to request an appearance on the show, and the man who worshiped them wasn't about to say no.)

This time, Bush was in even bigger trouble, as Clinton was threatening to bury him. Vice President Dan Quayle also came on the show. "One of our jobs was to rally the base," said Quayle press secretary David Beckwith to the *Tribune*, "and people who listen to Rush tend to be our base."

Of course, during the campaign, Rush couldn't resist a little levity to keep things rolling. One afternoon in late October, he shocked his audience by announcing a dramatic turnaround: "I can no longer ignore what is becoming obvious. I've decided to endorse Bill Clinton. It's necessary to have the courage to change," echoing the candidate's familiar campaign motto.

The dittoheads went berserk. What was happening to their Rush? If he loses it, then we're all in trouble. Some threatened to return copies of his book. Even a member of Bush's reelection campaign called EFM to express concern. "They were panicking," McLaughlin told the *Los Angeles Times*. "They said their phones were ringing off the hook."

Surely Rush was joking. Apparently not. For the first half hour, he flatly denied it. Finally, it was time to make his point. "How can you hold me to something I said seventeen minutes ago?" he told his listeners. "That was in the past." Then to the next caller: "That was twenty-three minutes ago. I never said that." Then he accused listeners of challenging his integrity and he denied having endorsed Clinton. "Can we look forward now?" he asked. "People want to keep looking into my past. How can you keep bringing up my past?"

Near the end of the show, he explained the hoax: "It just hit me this morning to do this," he told the *Los Angeles Times*. "Governor Clinton has been doing for 20 years what I did on my show today—saying things and denying them. The whole reason I'm a success is because people trust me and believe me. Character does matter, even for a lowly talk-show host, and it should even more for a presidential candidate." Rush said he staged a similar hoax once before, in 1990. "I tried to make people believe I had changed my mind and become a sensitive liberal."

Understandably, Rush, the sensitive conservative, has been seen by many as a possible future candidate for national office. If Buchanan could run, why not him? However, whenever the issue of politics comes around, Rush insists that he is a radio junkie, and that he's not even comfortable with the notion that he tries to influence elections. "I'm not a movement conservative," he told the *Washington Times*. "There's no agenda on this show. I'm not trying to register voters or impact policy." He told *Vanity Fair*: "My purpose is not to make America more like what I think it should be. My purpose is not to make more conservatives or register more Republicans, or to get invited to the White House for a state dinner, or any of those things. I simply want to be the best radio guy there is."

Hazlett said anyone who thinks Rush is on the fast track to gaining public office doesn't understand him. "Why would someone in Rush's position quit and run for office?" he said. "It would be a huge demotion ... he wouldn't be able to call his own shots anymore." Kit Carson, his chief of staff, said Rush could never be a politician because "the first thing you have to do is go out and ask for money," which he would never do.

Nonetheless, it can't be disputed that Rush thrives on his proximity to the inner corridors of power, and he certainly did not resist the temptation to get involved in the primary battle between Bush and Buchanan; he certainly did play politics with his show. Rush was overjoyed when Bush sent him a note thanking him for all the nice comments he made about him during the late stages of the election, and was thrilled when he thought Buchanan was on his way to the studio one day. Once, according to a newspaper account, during a commercial break when broadcasting from the 1992 Republican Convention in Houston, Rush remarked to an assistant: "On a roll here, Jimbo, on a roll. I'm in the vice president's box tonight."

21

RUSH NEVER FORGETS HIS FAILURES, AND ONE OF them was television. He knew that someday he would have to make up for the disaster on "The Pat Sajak Show," and for other ventures that never went anywhere. Then Roger Ailes came into his life, and Rush seized the opportunity.

Ailes was a Republican insider who had served as George Bush's television adviser in the 1988 presidential race, and had coached Reagan and Nixon. It had been Ailes who had help convince Bush to become the aggressor against the overmatched Michael Dukakis. Dukakis made the mistake of jumping into a tank. Bush brought Willie Horton into the spotlight. Ailes had also produced NBC's "Tomorrow," and the nationally syndicated "Mike Douglas Show." His company, Multimedia Entertainment, sold the talk shows of Phil Donahue and Sally Jessy Raphael. Sensing Limbaugh's potentially powerful appeal on the small screen, Ailes came to him in late 1990 with the idea of launching a new television show. Rush had always envisioned himself doing a cross between "MacNeil/Lehrer" and "The Tonight Show," and that's exactly what Ailes had in mind. "Rush has brains, a sense of humor and he's the best improvisational performer since Jack Paar," Ailes told *Newsweek*.

In September of 1992, the "Rush Limbaugh Show" made its debut on 183 stations covering ninety-five percent of the nation. During a rehearsal taping, the Rush on TV wasn't much different than the Rush on radio. "Let me ask you a question," he said, in typically blunt style. "How are things for you? Got two cars in the garage? Got your television on, obviously. And how fortunate you are to have me on it. How much better could life be? Are you sitting around thinking about slitting your wrists? Do you want to move to Somalia?"

From the start, he promised this would be a different kind of television show. "The afternoon talk shows are all the same and the late-night shows are all the same," he told the *Los Angeles Times*. "You've got a band. You've got celebrity guests and you've got, basically, conservative bashing: Make fun of Quayle. This is going to be one show in America where Quayle won't be made fun of."

Rush, of course, was well aware that because of his personality and message, he would have to get off to a good start. Affiliates wouldn't wait long to find a replacement. "The TV managers and the TV programmers are just as afraid as the radio guys were at first," he told the *Los Angeles Times*. "And they're going to say, 'This show's got to prove itself. We don't know what this guy's going to do. Oh my God, what kind of horror is going to be visited on America because of this guy?'"

Even people in Rush's inner circle, however, weren't sure whether his success on radio could translate well to television, including his brother. "The odds are against anyone in TV," David Limbaugh told the *Southeast Missourian*. "And he'll receive some resistance from advertisers who view his show as too controversial. It takes different talents to do radio and TV, and some people can do both. The question is if he has the talent to do both."

It didn't take long to find out. Rush's show, in some markets, fared better in the ratings than the talk shows hosted by David Letterman and Arsenio Hall, and trailed only "Nightline" and Jay Leno. In his first week, he garnered a 2.5 Nielsen rating and a 10 share nationwide. (About two million households tuned in each weeknight.)

Skeptics had wondered how anybody, even someone with Rush's charisma, could just sit at a desk and pontificate for a half hour on network television. One would have imagined clickers around the country switching to another channel. "They were letting him do the radio show with a camera," said Paratore, who had produced the failed television pilot with Rush and Gloria Allred. "But people started to watch it." Skeptics had also wondered whether advertisers would be willing to buy time on such a controversial conservative show.

Willing and able. *Electronic Media*, based on a survey of television station managers, determined that "Roseanne" and Rush were the "two most rewarding purchases" of 1992. Limbaugh's TV show can garner $24,000 per half minute from premium advertisers it reported. Once again, Rush had turned into gold.

Rush, however, wasn't thrilled at first with his television performances. He, too, wondered whether people would be satisfied just hearing him speak behind a desk. He also worried about his constant fidgeting. "I hated it. I hated the adjustment," he told the *Los Angeles Times*. "I hated me. I didn't think I was any good. I was mad at myself for not being able to be myself. I went out there and froze up. I didn't relax and let what I felt flow through me."

Over time, however, Rush's natural instincts as an entertainer overcame his initial hesitation, and the television show proceeded as smoothly as his radio program. His staff started to employ better graphics, news clippings, and video footage to make the show more entertaining. *Newsweek* summed it up best: "He's the American White Male under siege, coping with femi-Nazis, dolphin huggers, 'wacko' environmentalists and closet 'socialists' such as Bill Clinton." The publication also, however, expressed severe doubts about Limbaugh's staying power. "TV's far more intimate than radio, and its survivors are usually soothing figures like Johnny Carson," the magazine wrote, "not 'hot' personalities like Morton Downey, Jr., and Limbaugh."

But *Time* gave Rush a glowing review, yet another stamp of legitimacy from the mainstream press he tries so hard to alienate. "Rush has taken to the medium in no time flat," it said. ". . . He woos the camera like an avid freshman on a fluke date with the senior prom queen. He guffaws, he blusters, he bats his eyes, he makes kissy-face. He will do anything to keep you watching."

Some reviews, according to *Success*, weren't as complimentary. *Milwaukee Journal*: ". . . As disjointed and inept a half hour as TV offers." *Cleveland Plain Dealer*: "Like [being] stuck at a very bad party next to a disingenuously argumentative loudmouth who won't shut up even when his mouth is full of cheese dip." *Boston Globe*: "A nakedly exposed blowhard."

But, more important than media approval was the fact that the regular legion of dittoheads followed their hero to television. When one affiliate, Channel 8 in Dallas, contemplated dropping him from its late-night lineup, hundreds of fans jammed the switchboards, causing station executives to rethink their decision. Rush, as is his custom, gave out Channel 8's phone number on the air. Each time he needed to rally the troops, General Limbaugh only had to give the order. In the beginning, some stations, anxious to see how the television experiment would work, gave him poor time slots, but as the show got good reviews and strong ratings in the November sweeps period, he got upgrades on about twenty-five stations.

The Rush rooms also began to take off. At about a hundred restaurants across the country, in cities like Green Bay, Wisconsin, Albany, New York, and Jacksonville, Florida, for example, people started to come specifically to dine with fellow dittoheads. A typical establishment is the Grill N'Chill restaurant in Falmouth, Massachusetts. "I can usually spot them coming through the door," owner Ralph Rodrigues told the *Boston Globe*. "They're more intelligent looking, mostly younger types. Business people.

Not too many retirees, though." That description fits well into Rush's main audience: Men between twenty-five and fifty-four. According to *Success*, of Rush's adult audience, eighty-three percent have attended some college, while twenty percent have been to graduate school.

Rush had conquered radio. He had even made an unprecedented launch into television. He was one of the most entertaining speakers in the country. Only one more task remained. He had to do what everyone famous in America eventually does. He had to write a book. "My friends told me that if I wanted my views to be taken seriously," Rush told *Success*, "I had to write a book defending them. I'm not a writer. I'm a radio guy. But I take my beliefs with the utmost seriousness, and I want everyone else to."

So, in late 1991, with the help of *Wall Street Journal* editorial writer John Fund, Rush began the process of putting his thoughts on paper. Simon & Schuster gave him a six-figure advance. His fans couldn't wait.

Rush was proud to get an opportunity to show off his writing skills. In his acknowledgments to *The Way Things Ought To Be*, Rush claims he was determined that, despite the fact that his writing experience was limited, he was going to write it himself rather than "farming it out to a ghost writer." One problem: That is mostly what he did do. Fund taped their conversations, and then wrote the first draft from the transcriptions. After Fund completed the draft, Rush asked his brother to look at it and make some changes.

"He is a profound conservative thinker, and a much better writer than I will ever be," he wrote in the book's acknowledgments.

"I have no doubts that Rush Limbaugh could write a book," said Christine Craft, his familiar critic. "The difference is, he didn't. It's another example of pawning something off as something it's not."

But his fans didn't care whether Rush wrote the book or hired a ghost writer. Nor did they care that the vast majority of the book was merely regurgitations of the standard right-wing positions—abortion, the homeless, welfare, the environment, etc.—he has staked out hundreds of times on the air. They gobbled up the book almost faster than it could be printed. By the summer of 1993, the book had sold about 2.5 million copies, landing on the *New York Times* best-seller list for month after month, and threatening to surpass *Iacocca*, according to *Success*, as the most prolific-selling nonfiction hardcover of all time. The way things ought to be made plenty of sense to them.

The press, however, wasn't nearly as receptive. It was one thing to acknowledge The Rush Phenomenon, and prominently feature cover stories about him. It was quite another to endorse his agenda. The *Washington Post* called it a "disappointingly mean-spirited and oblivious vision of America. A cruel illusion." The *New York Times*, which reportedly didn't review it until after it had been on the best-seller list for *six* months, referred to it as a "rant of opinions, gags, and insults, with a few facts or near facts sprinkled in like the meat in last week's stew." The media were again where they belonged—assaulting Rush and everything he and his followers represented.

Attacks came from other corners, including, surprisingly enough, the Oval Office. In after-dinner remarks before twenty-four hundred people at the annual gathering of the White House Correspondents' Association in early May of 1993, President Clinton went after Rush. Clinton said that Limbaugh had come to the defense of Attorney General Janet Reno after the disastrous climax of the fifty-one day standoff against cult members in Waco, Texas, only "because she was attacked by a black guy." The president was referring to Rep. John Conyers, the black Michigan Democrat, who had suggested Reno should resign. Some members of the audience groaned at Clinton's remarks, and White House staffers said later that he regretted the comment.

Rush was in attendance and was certainly not going to waste this precious opportunity to play the victim. "I don't mind being thought of in an ill way by Bill Clinton," he told reporters, "but I'm not a racist. I'm the absolute furthest thing from a racist." The irony of the moment was inescapable. Here was Rush Limbaugh, the man who degraded women, homosexuals, the poor and the socially conscious environmentalists, and *he* was complaining about being offended.

On his radio show, Rush continued the part, mocking Clinton by saying it was he, not the president, who should apologize for his views. "He called me that night," said Hazlett. "He told me all these famous journalists had come up to him and said, 'Oh that's terrible, you can't let the president of the United States call you a racist.'" But Rush wasn't outraged by this. "He turned it around and made it a joke on Clinton, which it was."

So that is how far he had come from Cape Girardeau. Rush was the subject of a president's joke.

This year also saw him advance another step toward legitimacy when NBC News announced that on one Sunday, Rush would be the "alternative media" commentator on the roundtable portion of the show. "We can't be haughty about Limbaugh," said Tim Russert, NBC's Washington Bureau Chief told *Newsday*. "I'm sure, with Congress reconvening, he'll ask people to call their senators, to call their representatives."

Last May, Rush called for an unofficial dittohead convention. An estimated thirty-five thousand of that not-so-rare breed packed Old Town Square in Fort Collins, Colorado, to attend Dan's Bake Sale. The event was, in theory, held for Dan Kay, the twenty-four-year-old former flea market employee who had called Rush's show in March and said he couldn't afford the $29.95 for his newsletter, the *Limbaugh Letter*. (The monthly newsletter began in October 1992, and its circulation is already nearing 250,000. It features more of the same Limbaugh litany of opinions, along with an interview with a prominent conservative.)

In reality, though, the event was held to honor Rush. Billed as Rushstock '93, it was a chance for the Right to gather outdoors to celebrate *its* platform for America. Fans arrived in cars, planes, and tour buses from nearly every state to demonstrate their support of the sale Limbaugh had hyped on his show for two months. At more than eighty booths, vendors hawked T-shirts, buttons, mugs, bumper stickers, cookies and newsletters. One booth sold sweatshirts with Clinton-bashing phrases from Politically Incorrect Inc., a firm from Plymouth, Michigan.

Finally, Rush, accompanied by eight security officers, spoke to his disciples who had been waiting for hours. "I'm sorry I kept you waiting, but my barber was late," he said, in reference to Clinton's famous haircut aboard *Air Force One* in Los Angeles. Then, he got serious. "We are the majority of thinkers in the country," he said. "Stick to your principles, folks. They may fear you for that, but that's when you'll make your point."

Rush Hudson Limbaugh III, overcoming a series of professional and personal failures, had certainly stuck to his principles and now his points were inspiring millions of followers and making millions of dollars. He was the epitome of The American Dream, a chubby kid from Cape Girardeau, Missouri, who never surrendered his goal despite all the odds, who, more importantly, never surrendered himself. He is forty-two, and he hopes to never wake up.

Epilogue

SO WHO IS RUSH LIMBAUGH?

Is he a major conservative thinker? Is he a crafty capitalist? Is he a master entertainer?

He is all three in one. He took the deep-rooted convictions of his family and Midwest surroundings and blended them perfectly to fit the America of the 1990s. He knows the country is in peril, sick of legislative gridlock, moral decay, and media manipulation. He has told people that it's not their fault that everything is falling apart. He has identified the culprits, and been vigilant in making sure they take responsibility. He has become the voice for the new disenchanted, the hard-working, well-educated taxpayers who don't feel safe anymore, who believe somebody else is trying to take over their country. He is their last defender.

His conservative credentials can't be challenged. From abortion to gun control to gay rights, Rush is Right every time, no doubt more consistent to his constituents on the air than most politicians or protesters. "It is foolish," Ailes told the *Los Angeles Times*, "to believe that the conservative commentator's political views are not the core of his appeal." He counts as his heroes people like

Bill Bennett, George Will, and William F. Buckley, Jr., and you can't get much more conservative than that. "If people thought I didn't believe this stuff," Rush told Costas, "my credibility wouldn't be what it is. I wouldn't be able to endorse products . . . Look at the people who have had long legs. A lot are from the Midwest, and they're honest."

Yet at the same time, as Rush proudly admits, he likes to "push the envelope," consistently exaggerating his opinions to be as controversial and entertaining as possible. Does he really believe in everything he says? Of course not. This is radio, and Rush is a performer. Above anything else, he wants to be recognized as the best talk show host in the world. That takes precedence over winning any debates or personality polls. Some contend he would be just as popular if he were one of the "flaming libs" he likes to attack, and that might be true. He takes special delight in people not knowing when the act ends and the real Rush begins. "I hope the public never finds out," he once told the *Southeast Missourian*. "That's part of the mystique of radio. It's the theatre of the mind. I want people to always be guessing and wondering. The truth is the line between the personality and me is a fine line."

The real Rush, according to those who know him best, is private, subdued, more interested in listening than lecturing. Like any performer, he relaxes between appearances, gearing up for when the light goes on and Excellence in Broadcasting must begin again. If anything, strangely enough, he seems genuinely disturbed when he deeply offends anybody, and always hopes that his victims recognize his comments as more shtick than substance. When he first met his second wife, Michelle, and thought he had been rude, he quickly tried to fix it with an apology. When he felt he had hurt AIDS victims with his insensitive remarks, he quickly tried to fix it by donating $10,000 to the Pediatric AIDS Foundation.

He is also extremely generous. Kitty O'Neal, his former producer in Sacramento, said Rush gave her a "mammoth check" of $1,500 as a wedding gift. On another occasion, according to *Vanity Fair*, he picked up the $38,000 tab for a thank-you cruise for his staff, and gave them individual gifts. Louise Adams, his surrogate mother from the Royals, said Rush gave one of her daughters $1,000 for a wedding gift, and didn't even come to the ceremony. "He is a man capable of incredible kindness," said one ex-KFBK colleague. "He is very loyal and comes through for people."

Yet Rush is not satisfied. Each time he conquers one world, he immediately sets his sights on another, from public speaking to print to television, etc. It seems he is most interested in one goal—posterity. "I'm not riding the crest of a wave," he told the *New York Times* in March of 1993. "I'm going to stay hot as long as I want to stay hot, and that's directly relatable to how much passion I have about my work." He talks frequently on his show about the talents who prematurely exploited their audience, and then slipped quietly into obscurity.

He is keenly aware of all the doubters who assumed he would be another passing fad in America's short attention span, unable to withstand the most important challenge of them all: Time. There were those who speculated he could only thrive under a Republican president, and that perhaps the nation's mood toward him would change with the election of a liberal Democrat. Well, squash that theory. Bill Clinton became president and Rush became more popular. He has a more convenient target than ever. He starts each radio show by referring to the number of days the Clinton Administration has been in office, which is symbolic of how long America has been held hostage. Rush couldn't have asked for a better gift than a Bill Clinton victory. "I teased him last summer of engineering the Clinton victory," Hazlett said. The anti-Clinton forces used Rush as the "the lightning rod. It's an enviable position."

Nor is Rush happy. His on-air arrogance, as friends have noted, is obviously a mask for the deep insecurities he has experienced since adolescence. Struggling so many years to be accepted by his family for who he was—a son with headphones, not a law degree—Rush has, in a way, never quite believed in his accomplishments. "I have not changed a thing about my self-perception," he told *Vanity Fair* in 1992. "I still get up and read the New York papers and see my name not mentioned and think I'm a failure, that I'm not mattering, that nobody knows who I am in the city I live in, and it bugs me greatly. I just sit here and get depressed."

Mary McKenna, his news anchor from KMBZ, whom he called "lovely and gracious," on the air, said it best about the man who has become more famous than anybody else in radio.

"I think his first thing is to be loved," McKenna said. "Rush Limbaugh is insecure and wants to be loved. He wants to be put on a pedestal. He wants his listeners to hold him in high esteem. And if he makes money doing it, so be it."

MICHAEL ARKUSH, a staff writer for the *Los Angeles Times*, lives with his wife, Pauletta Walsh, and stepdaughter, Jade, in Pacific Palisades, California. Arkush, along with Steve Springer, cowrote *60 Years of USC-UCLA Football*.